Acknowledg

My life has been touched by so many amazing people and I want to acknowledge you all for being a part of my journey. I would not experience so much magic if it were not for you all.

My children are my life, I love you all so much. Dylan, I am so proud of the man you have become. Eithen, I love you to the moon and back, let's find your magic. Kiera, you are going to shine so bright in this life. Saoirse, you are a strong gifted girl who will do amazing things. Eimear, you are a rainbow shining into any dull day. Mary, your strength and determination is something I am in awe of.

To Kieran thank you for our children and for your love.

To my mum and dad thank you for being strong loving people who I can look up to in life.

To my sister Emma who is so smart, talented and giving. The best support ever!

To my sister Lisa, you are such a great mum not only to your kids but to everyone's. You know that every child deserves to be loved.

To my brothers who are building awesome lives for themselves.

To my Serenity Press partner and friend Monique, we make magic happen together. Thanks for being a very special person.

To my editor and friend Teena Raffa-Mulligan no words can express my gratitude but I hope that you know I treasure you so much.

To my beautiful friend Tess Woods who shines magic into many lives and writes amazing books. Thank you for our friendship I treasure it so much.

To Peace Mitchell and Katy Garner for gifting me a scholarship to their 2015 conference where I set the intention of being a speaker and award winning entrepreneur. Thank you for creating a loving platform for women in business to succeed in. And thank you for your love and friendship.

To Donna Di Lallo who has believed in me since the moment I put finger to keyboard, I would not be who I am today if it were not for your belief.

To Ida Jansson for being the best cover and interior designer ever. You have helped me be a more confident business person and author because I know I can rely on your magical vision. Thank you for being amazing.

To my new team of editors, illustrators, marketers, printers, designers and everyone who helps me create my empire so that I can give my best self to others, thank you so much.

To all of the Serenity Press authors, you are amazing. To all of my Publishing academy students and Making Magic Happen Academy students and authors thank you for choosing me to join you on your journey.

A huge thank you to Kate, Donna and Dianna and all of the other businesses at The Lab Factory for being amazing. I love being part of this awesome collaborative project.

To Michelle Sanchez for the amazing bio and website content for Karenmcdermott.com.au

To Rushelle Lister for being a consistent support and very special person.

Mindful MAGIC

K P WEAVER

Copyright © 2020 K P WEAVER

First published in Australia in 2020
by MMH PRESS

www.mmhpress.com

All rights reserved. No part of this book may be used or reproduced by any means, graphic, electronic, or mechanical, including photocopying, recording, taping or by any information storage retrieval system without the written permission of the copyright owner except in the case of brief quotations embodied in critical articles and reviews.

This is a work of fiction. Names, characters, businesses, places, events and incidents are either the products of the author's imagination or used in a fictitious manner. Any resemblance to actual persons, living or dead, or actual events is purely coincidental.
National Library of Australia Cataloguing-in-Publication data:
Mindful Magic/Making Magic Happen Academy
Romance – fiction

Editor: Teena Raffa-Mulligan
Cover and interior designer: Ida Jansson

ISBN 978-0-6488031-0-2 (sc)
ISBN 978-0-6488031-1-9 (e)

This book is dedicated to my mum.
Thank you for showing me that anything is possible.

I can easily prioritise what matters for my greater good.

To all of my readers, without you all writing would not be so magical.

To Tracy, Sheena and all of my supportive readers in Ireland. You know who you are thank you so much.

And lastly thank you to the Universe for gifting me everything I could ever want in this lifetime.

When I need to I can enter my inner zone.

CONTENTS

Introduction	**15**
Magic Mindfulness	**19**
Early mindset experiences	25
Mindset and fear	27
Thought awareness	**33**
First step Attraction	37
Mindful Task	**39**
Instant mindset shifters	**43**
Section 1: Mindful Magic	**47**
Power of Thought	47
Live your dream now, not in the future	52

Mighty Mindset	55
Exercise	59
Notes	61

Section 2: Perspective Power — 63

Peripheral perspective	65
Anything is possible	67
Key to a magic mindset	69
Exercise	71
Notes	75

Section 3: Kindness Kick — 77

Part A. Kind energy	77
Part B. If like attracts like, kind attracts kind.	79
Part C. Why kindness will get you far.	81
Exercise	83
Notes	85

Section 4: Live Love — 87

Part A: Law of love	87
Part B: Love, the healer	90
Part C: Let all that you do be done in love	93
Exercise	95
Notes	97

Section 5: Confident Cash — 99

    Part A: Absolute abundance — 99

    Part B: Money Mindset — 102

    Part C: Money is on its way — 104

    Exercise — 106

    Notes — 108

Section 6: Intuitive Intention — 111

    Part A: Power of intention — 111

    Part B: Fabulous focus — 113

    Part C: Journal progress — 115

    Exercise — 117

    Notes — 119

Final: Great Thinkers — 121

Quotes to live by — 125

Summary — 127

Collection of articles — 131

    Our Universal Minds — 131

    The Spiritual Law of Attraction — 136

    Loving Law of Attraction: The Mirror Effect — 140

    Loving Law of Attraction: A tortoise or a hare? — 143

    Loving Law of Attraction: Ask – Believe – Receive — 145

    Anything is possible, you just have to believe. — 147

Loving Law of Attraction: A negative path	150
Loving Law of Attraction: To catch a fish!	153
Go within or go without	157
The Knowing	**163**

I alone am in control of my thoughts and emotions.

When you understand that there is a power greater than you can ever imagine and it's there to serve you. That's a powerful realisation.

KAREN MCDERMOTT

INTRODUCTION

Take a look at the cover of this book. Mindfulness is all about having your peripheral vision switched on to allow the magic in and be aware what to shield yourself from. The gold circle is you in all of your magnificent glory, the circumference is what it is like to be mindful. It is beautiful, blocking out what doesn't serve your greater good yet open to letting in the most magical gifts. This is a magical state, one that serves YOU and your highest potential. Stay connected to this state of consciousness and there is nothing that cannot be achieved.

Approach it from a loving perspective and watch how fast it comes. We all have this primitive power but it has been lost throughout generations. There are some though who are gifted and this comes from a menagerie of circumstance and inbuilt soulful ability. It is there at birth and if nurtured every child will have the opportunity to reach their highest self.

I have always shone, it comes naturally, but I am also quite humble and empathetic. It is just who I am and I embrace it. I was blessed to have been raised totally surrounded by love. My biggest memory of childhood is the feeling of being loved one hundred per cent unconditionally. This is the greatest gift any parent can give their child. I have discovered life lessons don't necessarily have to be imposed; they will be learned throughout the journey. But when you gift a child the safety of knowing what it is to be loved they will always know that they are. It is in this very *Knowing* that hope resides. Hope is a powerful resource for the journey of life.

In this book you will learn about the power of intention and how to reach your highest potential. The seven sections all come with an exercise and note section that you can dip in and out of. But of course the best results will come from focused loving energy.

You have been guided to this book for a reason, a reason you may not know yet. The concept of Mindful Magic may seem unachievable for you right now. It is one hundred per cent achievable for everyone and the first point to check off the list is belief. You do deserve to reach your highest potential, no matter what your circumstance or position in the world. Everyone has the power within, it is time to harness it in love and let it serve you now. There is no need to live a life of regrets. Your intuition will guide you along the right path.

- Do three things every day to work towards your goal.
- Focus on the positives.
- Connect with the most powerful feeling of all…the feeling that opens channels to your heart's desire – love.

For me this feeling often channels through gratitude. As I sit here and write this my children are snuggled up in bed safe and sound and all I feel is love flowing from every cell in my body. I know that today is going to be fabulous because I have begun it doing the thing I love most, which is writing and inspiring others. When my kids wake each morning I will give them all a snugly hug and our day will begin. I am grateful to live such a blessed life. I shut out all things that are not positive and I embrace the beauty in every day.

Be thankful for what you have, you'll end up having more. If you concentrate on what you don't have, you will never ever have enough.

OPRAH WINFREY

MAGIC MINDFULNESS

Do you believe in magic? This is a big question to ask yourself, because if your answer is 'no' then the Law of Attraction cannot make sure you experience magic in your life. However, if you answer 'yes' then the Law of Attraction MUST deliver a magical life to you.

I believe in the magic of life. Do you? I also realise that the essence of making it work is to be mindful of the energy we emit into the world because it is responsible for what is attracted to us. I liken it to a magnetic frequency that attracts other frequencies our way and what we put out is what we get back. It makes sense to be mindful of what we are putting out there. At first it is a hard concept, but it can be learned.

I hope that through my words you will see things from a clearer perspective and understand the potential of the magic you can create.

This book has been written through the channel of love, knowledge and experience of three important life-enhancing areas, the Law of Attraction, trialing the theory and the loving intention.

I am passionate about helping others to have a better experience of the one precious life they have. So when I was asked to write this book I made time for it to happen.

Our mindset is a powerful tool. It is responsible for our experience of life so why do we not invest more time learning how to navigate it to our advantage? Shifting only one simple thought pattern has the potential to have a profound impact on our lives. When we explore things we accept to be fact, we can often discover limiting beliefs that don't serve us anymore.

Magic happens when we believe.

You limit reaching your highest potential because it is a human inbuilt mechanism to protect and stay safe and these beliefs are programmed in our minds. The reality is that we have the power to reprogram any mindset. Couple this with connecting to the power of *Knowing* and we will discover new heights that we could only have dreamt of before. I think I was born connected to my *Knowing*. My mother always said I had a mind of my own. I was always happy when she said it, even though I imagine it was quite challenging at times raising me with my headstrong ways. But as the saying goes, *if you have the courage to let your child grow freely they may just change the world.* I was blessed with the freedom to make my own mistakes and learn the lessons from them and I never make the same mistake twice. My parents were stricter with my younger sisters because I had pushed most of the boundaries to the limits and they weren't gifted the freedom I had.

It is now time to get excited about your potential.

In this book I will show you how to discover and live your best life. You all have one waiting for you to find. Do you ever watch others living their true calling, wondering why yours has eluded you?

My intention for writing these words is to connect with as many people as possible to show them that magic is possible in their lives. If I can have a magical life, anyone can.

I have outlined a structure for this book but as with most things I undertake in my life I will allow the freedom of organic thoughts to flow throughout. I have purposely left them in so you can absorb the gems of wisdom woven through the words that flow from purpose.

> 'Start to observe your thoughts – repeated thoughts become beliefs which become stories which are collated in the mind to form a mindset! Find out what word you may be telling yourself and how it may be affecting you.'
>
> *Amanda Gore*

There are seven sections, each with three parts. Each section includes an exercise relevant to the topic. In the final chapter I explore other great thinkers who make magic happen through their thoughts. Through other people's ideologies we can learn so much and often their gift to us is the permission to think alternatively. At the end there is a bonus section with articles I wrote while studying the Law of Attraction.

Many of us are taught to do things *the right way*. The problem is that often conforming to this 'right way' is not aligned with our purpose or it doesn't allow us the freedom we need to explore the magic of life. Creative practices are often frowned upon even though they offer a safe haven for release, self expression and facilitate deep connections with others.

A historical piece that did the rounds on Facebook recently shared bizarre reasons for women to be admitted to a mental asylum from 1864 to 1889. It was deemed reasonable for someone to be admitted to a mental asylum if they desired to read a novel or if their husband abused them. How about that for mindset! That was not so many generations ago and it does take a few generations for the remnants of outdated ideologies to be completely dispelled. I use it as an example because it shows firsthand the extent to which mindsets can change throughout evolution and through some cultures, some moving forward faster than others.

I have discovered that quite often restrictions on the freedom of the mind often stem from fear of the possibilities and of the powers not being in control. It is easier to mould a nation into what can be controlled. I totally understand that is required when it comes to evil thoughts but not when thoughts have a true loving intention of growth and exploration.

In the book *The Secret* by Rhonda Byrne she reveals how the power of our minds was so feared that it was hidden and discouraged in many religions. It was in fact coveted! I was fascinated to discover the ancient Babylonians believed in the law of tithing. I like this law as it involves giving one tenth of all money or riches to other people. The Law is built upon the mindset that if you give, you will receive and what we can learn from the ancient Babylonians is that when this law is in full practice it is aligned with the frequency of abundance.

It feels good to give and that good feeling is an actual energy that emits a vibration that will also connect with the gratitude vibration from the person receiving. There is a lot of positive energy in this interaction so only good things can come from it.

So all we have to do is change our whole perspective on taxation. For this to work, we need to feel good that we are helping make wonderful things happen in our country by paying tax, and in return the government needs to be grateful to each and every tax payer. This ideology may have a way to go but we can all do our bit. In the same way as forgiving someone because it gives us freedom, we can feel good about paying our tax to gain as much potential as possible from the flow of available abundance, which is for our greater good.

It's a good feeling to help someone out so give when you can and feel good about it. If you are on the receiving end, be grateful for everything you receive, don't push things away. Pay it forward if the gift is not for you because by saying 'no' you are closing the door on the flow.

> 'If you are thinking, "I will give when I have enough money," then the tithing law says you will never have enough money, because you have to give first.
> Many of the wealthiest people on the planet tithed their way to wealth, and they have never stopped tithing!'
> *Rhonda Byrne*

We can all give. I always give without expectation and receive so much in return. Maybe that is a key to my success as the feeling is sure to be on a frequency of receiving from the universe. We all have the capacity to give. If we adjust our mindset to think that by giving we are not losing, we are in fact winning because what you give will return to you tenfold if you give with the truest of intention.

> 'No one has ever become poor from giving.'
> *Anne Frank*

After years of nothing but dullness there was so much light. Since my arrival in Australia I have written more than twenty books, founded the most wonderful publishing company and had four beautiful daughters. Life is good and I am very grateful indeed.

When I found the place on this earth that I called my new home, something shifted in me. I had this feeling of *Knowing* that

I was in exactly the right place for me. Logically to other people I wasn't, but it felt so right that I was in the right place for me at the right time of my life and that is what mattered. I was ready for my new life to begin. Not once did I ever waver from the *Knowing* that I was to see through my journey to the other side of the world. The fact I was thirty-five weeks pregnant didn't faze me. That is a true example of trusting the feeling of *Knowing*. The feeling soon became something I trusted and instantly felt when something was right for me. It was and still is my true guide. When I don't know or I don't have the feeling of one hundred per cent yes then I say no or put off the decision-making process until I have more clarity. This is something I had to learn as I was a yes person, I had what Oprah refers to as a *disease to please*.

It's great to become aware that there is lots of magic surrounding us in every moment of every day. It is empowering to learn how to tap into it by becoming more aware. It is such a tragedy that so many people miss the magical signs of the universe because they are seeking something that is not aligned for them. Something they think they want without truly understanding the concept of *Knowing*.

One of the most important things I teach is that a *Knowing* is not a thinking thing as it may first be perceived; it is in fact a feeling thing that you do not waver from. When you have the ability to connect with your *Knowing* and have the unwavering trust and belief that it is working one hundred percent for you and your greater good, it is then you can move confidently in the *Knowing* that the universe has got your back, no matter what. That confidence has power beyond imagination, that power is a gift. We all have the wiring in place to connect to the *Knowing* feeling, but sadly some of us choose not to connect.

> 'The world is full of magic things, patiently waiting
> for our senses to grow sharper.'
> W B Yeats

Early mindset experiences

I was blessed with a childhood where I felt safe to explore life and its potential. Even though I grew up in Northern Ireland during the time of the troubles, when soldiers walked around with guns and bomb scares were daily occurrences, my parents' mindset was of acknowledging the fear but choosing to allow us a non-fear-based platform to grow from. I remember feeling loved unconditionally and that type of love gives you a super powerful mindset – Superpower.

You may not have the power to control where you begin your life, but you do have the power to choose where you live it.

Briefly use the space below to share your childhood feeling experience. (Hugs to anyone who needs one right now).

'The difference between how magical life felt when you were a child and how your life might be now is because you stopped believing in the magic of life.'
Rhonda Byrne

I am mindful of the impact of my words on others.

Mindset and fear

Often parents (and I am one of the guilty ones) instill fears in their children to protect them from the potential dangers they may face in life. If my child has not listened to my reasonable explanation about why they should not run off then I will talk about the 'Boogy Man'. I never thought I would ever share such tales and in fact I was very much against it until I had girls! But it is amazing the personal boundaries you will surpass with each child you have. My girls are more adventurous and push the boundaries way further than my boys ever did. With six children you have to instill something to make them think twice and the Boogy Man worked so the Boogy Man it is.

Something that fascinated me about the extent to which a mother would go to lovingly protect her daughters was the discovery of the reason behind the lack of a mother figure in fairytales. It is because it was often the mothers who made up the stories to help their daughters become more resilient should they ever be taken away or lose their life. Growing up in Ireland meant I was very familiar with traditional fairytales.

A beautiful story comes to mind about my late dear friend Geraldine. I worked in a factory in my late teens to mid-twenties and one of my good friends in there was a real storyteller, I could listen to her forever. One day she told us the true story of how she and her sister made everyone believe they had real fairies at the bottom of the garden. They were so convincing that they made the front page of a 1970s Irish national newspaper at the time. She knew how to tell a story. One about a beautiful red-haired girl had the hair on the back of my neck standing on end when I was driving the Irish backroads from Crom Castle twenty years later!

It is when I am gifted with a deeper insight that I sit up and think differently. I love challenging my thought patterns and understand that most things have a deeper meaning that gifts us a greater understanding than what is perceived at face value. Everyone can benefit from being mindful of their rigid thought patterns for flexibility gifts freedom.

Fear can be limiting and as a mum, I can see why these stories were created. These fears are instilled with loving intention but they can limit our potential. Freedom of the mind can be deemed reckless but I would like to challenge that mindset by suggesting it is reckless of us to waste our lives conforming to the limitations of fear. How can we discover our magic when we reside in our comfort zone with walls of fear surrounding us?

Feel the fear and do it anyway.

Elizabeth Gilbert often talks about fear and her book *Big Magic* explores creative living beyond fear.

> 'Yes you absolutely do need your fear, in order to protect you from actual dangers…But you do not need your fear in the realm of creative expression.'
> *Elizabeth Gilbert*

I went to listen to her at the Perth International Arts Festival in 2015. It felt strange for me to leave my young family to go out in the city on my own but I felt compelled to do so. I had touched base with Elizabeth on her Facebook page and she responded graciously that she would see me there. Of course I had hoped for a shout out but that didn't happen. Coincidentally there was a microphone set up at the stage beside my seat and yes, I shamelessly stated my seat number in the Facebook comment! But when she invited people to come forward to ask questions I refrained from the opportunity and didn't know why, because usually I would have been onto that straight away. Then the reason found me. After the event was over I was leaving via a side entrance and in a serendipitous moment I met her there. We exchanged a few words but it was her energy I connected with. I felt a familiar frequency from her to the one I had within myself, one comprised of magic. I instantly knew why I didn't get up during the event. This was to be our connection; it wasn't verbal, it was energy and I found the courage to open my shielded heart and brave the world again in that moment.

When time and circumstance align, magic happens.

Afterwards, empowered by the inspired interaction with Elizabeth Gilbert, I opened up my peripheral power and began to take action fully connected to the faith in my *Knowing*.

We all have the navigation tool required to discover our destiny. It is the most valuable tool in the universe and yet it costs nothing. There are those who think too much about how to find it, whereas it is the special knowing feeling that helps us to open up our heart core and allow the light to shine into our lives. I have been accessing it for years and I am blessed with the instant ability to connect.

> '*Sometimes we have to ponder life to discover the answers we are searching for.*'
> *Bella Blue*

Many people pay for mentors to help them find their answers when some stillness can gift us clarity. Follow that with some mindfulness and it can be enough to change anyone's life.

A little about my journey inward

Have you ever heard the saying *Go within or go without*? I wrote an article about it when I was evolving and it is included in my book *Heart Writer* and also in the back of this book.

I went through a pretty rough time during the second half of 2006 and all of 2007. I suffered Post Traumatic Stress Disorder (PTSD) and it totally altered my perspective on life. I became an introvert and this was totally the opposite of who I was. It is such a cliché but I was as low as I could possibly go and from there the only way was up.

So when more than a year later I endured something that shook me to my core I didn't know if I could handle the heartache. Losing my twin pregnancy was the most painful thing I have ever endured in my life. The pain of that loss was a physical pain, one that I will never forget. It pierced through my every thought, my heart was broken but it woke me up. I could feel again! I cried rivers of tears, for the babies I would never hold and for the year and a half of my life that I could never get back. I began to realise things that I never fully understood before. It was as if the whole time I was focused within was not wasted after all, it was a time when I observed life. I became more aware of the smaller things in life, I felt more knowledgeable.

I liken this time of my life to the metamorphosis of a butterfly. I was once a colourful caterpillar consuming as much as I could before I went into a cocoon where I lay still going through the motions of life until the time when I could release myself from the darkness of the cocoon and begin to live again.

I realised it was not my fault I was put in that situation, it was beyond my control, but it was my choice how I chose to deal with it. At that time in my life I needed to go within and this incident guided me there but I had overstayed my time and so I had to wake up. This realisation empowered me, it clicked a switch and I had my power back. What had shaken me to my core was that I didn't feel safe, I didn't feel in control of my own life, and that's not a nice feeling at all for it takes away your liberty and self-worth.

Since then my life has been the way I would have only ever dreamt of before. We got pregnant the next month, we were granted a visa to go to Australia, we got married and we emigrated to the other side of the world.

Mindfulness is not about changing who you are, it's about enhancing the experience of being you.

KAREN MCDERMOTT

THOUGHT AWARENESS

Being aware of your thoughts is the first major step towards creating a live you will love.

Our thoughts create our reality. They are responsible for the energy we emit. They are responsible for what we put out into the world and how others perceive us. They are all powerful. So it makes sense that we should be in control of them, right?

Mindfulness is the most natural way to control your thoughts. Being aware of what is happening around you is common sense! Then why do more of us not embrace it? Does it go against our human nature? Have we grown so far away from a mindful mindset that it takes a total conscious mind shift to help us find the perfect flow?

I am fascinated by how our minds work and especially how powerful they are. Our perceptions of life and the things that go on around us are often not aligned with where we want to be in life and so often you can feel unsettled, as if everything is against you or you just don't feel fulfilled.

If you can master your own thoughts and influence the thoughts of others, that's when you can make a REAL change.

I was intrigued by the psychology of *The Secret* when it swarmed the globe ten years ago. I read it in 2010, two years after moving to Australia. It was exactly what I needed to read at that moment in my life. I totally believe that when a book finds you at exactly the right time it shifts something within and your perspective on your world will not be the same again. This is a good thing when you are going against your flow, like I was. It was exactly what I needed to assist me in adjusting my perspective.

On paper I had the nice life. I was living the Irish dream of moving to Australia and at the time we had two boys and two girls but it seemed that every time I started to shine again something would drag me back. Why?

I couldn't see it then but I can clearly see now.

I wasn't living for me, I was living for others! I gave one hundred per cent to my family and didn't keep anything for myself. Anything I did try to salvage for myself was taken away by my hubby, who was highly stressed and didn't see why I should be happy if he was sacrificing all of himself for his family. I bore the weight of this for many years and sometimes I felt empathetic and the fixer in me wanted to help.

Then I discovered I was the one who had the power to change things. I didn't need to be a victim of circumstance. I had a right to be happy if that's what I chose to be, in fact ALL of my family would benefit from a happier me. My perspective began to shift and I began keeping some focus on me. I love being there for my family, it is one of my non-negotiables. I love being their carer, I love their hugs, I love their little noses and when they have grumpy faces. I love it when they shine and I love it when I have to nurse them back to health, I love all of this because I am a mum. But what kind of mother am I if I choose to sacrifice all of myself? I resolved that I would begin incrementally to pursue my dream. A dream that my childhood did not gift me the belief in achieving, but somehow the belief found me and ignited a strong passion inside me.

I now have the benefit of seeing in my children's eyes that they too know that if they want something, they can go get it! But they also value how hard you may need to work. I am happy to gift my children this. This is important to me. But it may not have been had I chosen to remain quiet, to play it safe. I chose to be brave and go forth to claim my dreams and you can too. You might not have to sacrifice as much as you think because others will see the passion burning inside you and make way for that magic to take hold.

Let everything you do be done in love.

This quote is the best piece of advice I can gift to anyone choosing to make magic happen in their lives. When I began studying The Law of Attraction I was beyond delighted to discover it was first called The Law of Love – a big 'Aha!' moment for me.

Take a moment to think about it. Look at the people making a difference in our world – Oprah, Mother Theresa, Elizabeth Gilbert, Louise Hay, Joanne Fedler, Peace Mitchell are a few on my list. These people have set aside any dependency on financial gain and opened their hearts to the world. They are brave yet they have pursued their heart-centred purpose with such intensity that we all feel the benefits and come to love them back, even though we may never have met them. We feel their energy directly. We trust them so we allow them into our hearts. Imagine a life where we could have our hearts open all of the time. Imagine how brave you need to be. Imagine how liberating it is.

I want you to think for one moment…what have you got

to lose? I suggest you have nothing to lose and so much to gain.

It comes down to a feeling of *Knowing*. Once you set an intention it is your job to switch on your peripheral power and become good friends with the *Knowing* feeling. It is your guide! It will never let you down. Through this inbuilt personal navigation tool you will always stay on the right path that serves your greater good. We all have one, but quite often we don't know how to use it. I will be gifting my children the insight on how to use theirs – no batteries needed!

Knowing is not a thinking thing, it is a feeling thing – make it your best friend.

First step Attraction

Asking the Universe for something is the first step and it's the easy part– but the real thing you should be considering is if you are really ready to receive all that you are asking the Universe for. We are human after all and sometimes we can send signs to the Universe that we want something we are not physically, mentally or emotionally prepared to actively receive.

Asking for something is one thing, receiving it is another. I wrote about this subject in my second novel *The Wish Giver*. Five people were visited by the Wish Giver and each had sacrifices to make to allow them to receive their request. It was written on the principle that things shift around you to give you what you ask for and sometimes what you have to sacrifice isn't worth it.

To receive something, there has to be inspired action and conviction that you really want to receive. No matter what it is you want to manifest you must first consider what you may be sacrificing in the pursuit of your dream.

To receive money, you have to exert effort to receive it because that is simply how things work. The Law of Attraction never fails us – it gives us exactly what we want deep in our hearts.

So if you want something, you really have to break down your emotional and mental defences to allow your dreams to manifest in physical reality. You have to let the Universe know you are ready to receive it. You receive what you have the courage to believe.

> 'To accomplish great things we must not only act, but also dream; not only plan, but also believe.'
> *Anatole France*

You become what you think about.

NAPOLEAN HILL

MINDFUL TASK

Before we begin I would like you to write a sentence in response to each of these questions.

What is mindfulness?

_____

What is magic?

_____

Mindfulness is not about changing who you are, it's about enhancing the experience of being you. Don't compromise yourself in your pursuit of success.

I can share with you the definitions of Mindfulness and Magic but I want you to define what they mean to you, right now in this very moment.

Before I continue I want to share with you why I wrote this book. I am passionate about the importance of what makes us pursue our dreams; our 'why' is a powerful essence in our journey.

One speech I connected with on a deep level was Matthew McConaghy's 2014 Oscar acceptance speech for Best Actor in *Dallas Buyers Club* when he spoke of three things he needed each day. I suggest you watch it as you will feel the emotion of its delivery. Words delivered through the heart channel reach down and nourish our soul, leaving a lasting impact, something to be mindful of.

> 'One, I need something to look up to, another is something to look forward to, and another is someone to chase.'
> *Matthew McConaghy*

The speech has so much impact because he is truly living his calling in exactly the way he chooses to and without compromising the beliefs at the root of his being. He emphasises the need for us to follow our dreams but not to compromise too much of ourselves in the pursuit.

It really struck a chord with me because I am passionate about the same thing. I am always mindful that although I push boundaries I will always maintain a balance between my priorities of family, work and play. This is a key to maintaining a successful mindset and manifesting successfully in the long term.

I have learnt a lot about manifesting and tested it many times. I do however have some non-negotiables that I don't jeopardise in pursuit of my calling. One of my best pieces of advice to you is to connect with yourself wholeheartedly. Every action has a reaction. Once you open the doors to receiving, amazing things will come your way. That is why I fuse mindfulness with the magic of manifesting. When you have that balance right, you will have few regrets. You will maintain your personal essence, the fundamental characteristic that makes you wonderfully you. If you keep that close at heart you will never go wrong. It will call you back at times on the journey so be sure to listen and check back in, its intention is to protect your greater good. Aspire to be the best version of you.

Definition of Mindfulness

The quality or state of being conscious or aware of something.
Cambridge English Dictionary

Definition of Magic

The use of special powers to make things happen that would usually be impossible.
Cambridge English Dictionary

When time and circumstance align, magic happens.

KAREN MCDERMOTT

INSTANT MINDSET SHIFTERS

Did you know that it takes three weeks to create a habit? You may read this fact a few times throughout this book but it is such an amazing piece of information to have instilled in your mind that I treat it as Gold.

There have been many occasions in my life when I have used this mindset to make dramatic changes. And somehow my mind allows me permission to make a dramatic change if it believes it only has to make the conscious effort for a few weeks. But of course after those three weeks of dedication your mind should have a new habit that feels more normal to execute.

I do this often when I am changing an eating habit. The first three weeks are so tough but after that, if I continue to make the right choices then it is much easier. It was the same when I gave up smoking. I loved it so much but for the greater good of my unborn baby I stopped and have never smoked again, but the first three weeks were the hardest. When I joined my first NaNoWriMo in 2010 it took three weeks to really find my flow of writing 1667 words every day but I did and that month I wrote a 50000 word novel, *The Visitor*. And believe me if I can make a life change in three weeks then so can you.

In those three weeks affirmations are really helpful. Below are some other possibilities.

- Affirmations
- Count to 10 before acting
- Three weeks of mindfulness
- Have a mindful reset button
- A mindset stone
- Mindful moments

Affirmations that are relevant to focusing your mindset on what you want to achieve can be very powerful. Whether it be money, happiness or health these little mind tricksters will make a real difference. Find affirmations that are relevant to what you want to achieve.

Counting to ten gives you time to think before you react. It's amazing how differently things can look ten seconds after you would have initially reacted. That space can gift the magic of clarity and avoid any regrettable actions that could arise.

The three weeks of mindfulness is a life-changing approach to instigating change or achieving goals.

Having a mindful reset button can reboot your mindset back to a more focused one clear of clutter.

I love having a mindset stone in my pocket or purse. I rub it and it has the power to instantly shift my energy. My stone of choice is a rose quartz, which is the love stone. You could look at different stones and see what resonates with you, because they all emit energy. Any stone will do though and when you have chosen your stone, sit with it and think of something that makes you feel good. Then when you touch the stone, feel that feeling and it will assist you in mindfully attracting magic into your life.

And finally, mindful moments. As we all have phones with us these days it is easy to have access to *mindful moments*. The way it works is to set your alarm with a nice tone to sound at different times throughout the day that work in with your schedule. When you hear the alarm you will feel good and that will reset your energy from what you have wound yourself into during that day. For the duration of the alarm going off, feel, feel, feel every magical tingle.

Mix and match these mindset shifters to work in with your life.

As soon as you start to feel differently about what you already have, you will start to attract more of the good things, more of the things you can be grateful for.

JOE VITALE

SECTION 1:
MINDFUL MAGIC

Power of Thought

If you want Magic to be a part of your life you must first believe in Magic.

Your thoughts are all powerful. They are energy and therefore instigate a reaction. Energy is what activates your energy field so be mindful of the thoughts that stream from your mind to your brain stem, instigating your nervous system to release a reaction out into your energy field.

Your energy field is strongest in close proximity.

Your energy field has the power to attract and deflect and is owned by your thoughts that are the creators of your feelings.

Every action causes a reaction.

The psychology behind the power of mindset can be difficult to comprehend with a closed mind, but when you open yourself up to possibilities anything can occur. My first experience of The Law of Attraction was through Rhonda Byrne's book *The Secret*. This book gifted me a deeper understanding of how powerful we all are. We are most definitely more than our body. The energy we create manifests our reality. I was intrigued by the knowledge and the 'Aha!' moments I had while reading this book. Everything made sense to me, it was as if my mind had opened wider than I could ever have imagined. I wanted to learn more, I needed to know more of this gold, it was totally aligned with how I wanted to think, totally aligned with what I knew to be.

> **'There is a truth deep down inside of you that has been waiting for you to discover it, and that truth is this: You deserve all good things life has to offer.'**
> *Rhonda Byrne, The Secret*

So too with Louise Hay's book, *You Can Heal Your Life*. The introduction to how powerful your mindset is in creating your health in a metaphysical sense is much less confronting than *The Secret* and yet just as powerful. This book also introduced me to the power of affirmations as an instant mind shift tool, enabling us to instantly connect with words that will trick our mind into initiating an emotion that is more aligned with our purpose, our health goals and ourselves.

There are no limits, only those we impose on ourselves.

We are all different and we all think differently! This is fabulous as can you imagine how bland the world would be if we were all the same? Variety is the spice of life! However, there is this universal law that is supported on a metaphysical level. What Louise Hay showed me is that I can shift my energy even if I am having a crap day or going through a rough time. I am in control of how to mindfully shift my energy and how I react. She taught me to be gentle with this new insight. She gifted me the power of affirmational knowledge. By saying something and feeling this power we can shift the power of our reality, thus shifting its outcome.

I recited this list of affirmations by Louise Hay every day when I was evolving. It helped me feel safe and trust that I was moving forward into my true self.

Deep at the centre of my being there is an infinite well of love.

I now allow this love to flow to the surface.

It fills my heart, my body, my mind, my consciousness, my very being, and radiates out from me in all directions and returns to me multiplied.

The more love I use and give, the more I have to give, the supply is endless.

The use of love makes me feel good; it is an expression of my inner joy.

Yes, I love myself, therefore I take loving care of my body.

I lovingly feed it nourishing food and beverages.

I lovingly groom it and dress it and my body lovingly responds to me with vibrant health and energy.

I love myself, therefore I provide for myself a comfortable home, one that fills all of my needs and is a pleasure to be in.

I fill the rooms with the vibration of love so that all who enter, myself included, will feel this love and be nurtured by it.

I love myself so I work at a job that I truly enjoy doing, one that uses all of my talents and abilities, working with and for people that I love and love me, and earning a good income.

I love myself, therefore I behave in a loving way to all people for I know that that which I give out returns to me multiplied.

I only attract loving people into my life for they are a mirror of what I am.

I love myself therefore I forgive and totally release the past and all past experiences and I am free.

I love myself therefore I love totally in the now, experiencing each moment as good and knowing that my future is bright and joyous and secure, for I am a beloved child of the Universe and the Universe lovingly takes care of me now and forever more.

And so it is.

Do you feel the energy in those words? Even typing this for you now opens up my heart and I feel that glow again. It brings me right back to a place where I had to have courage and trust that the changes I was implementing in my life were for the greater good of me and my young growing family.

These words also helped me tap straight into the most powerful energy of all – loving intention.

I would like to share with you a story about something that happened around this time. I was invited to a guided meditation with my beautiful forever friend, Donna. As a mum of a young family I rarely left my children so I could do things in the evening. I don't know why but on this occasion I felt as though I had to go, so with no expectation I arrived at the beautiful home of the person leading the meditation. It was my first ever meditation but oh my goodness what we all witnessed and felt through me was unbelievable.

The room had a beautiful energy. There were four of us there that night. I sat closest to the door and after a friendly chit chat we were guided into a meditation. I am not good at calming my mind, it is always active, but I did try, not knowing what I was supposed to be thinking, or not thinking for that matter, so I decided to listen to the tape that was playing. It was the voice of a man of Oriental origin. His words were calm, clear and powerful, they entrapped me straight away and I was being brought deep within myself. He worked from the busy mind, right down the face, neck and chest and stopped at the heart, where he talked about opening up the protective shield and feeling safe to let the love flow. WOW, WOW, WOW! A physical rush pulsated from my heart and I could feel the energy pulsating from my body so intensely. I felt like an electric pole radiating. I connected this feeling to the heart rushes I had sought medical attention for in previous months. This release was so intense it brought me to tears. The realisation was clear: I am a loving person and I had been protecting myself from living a love-filled life because of fear and circumstance.

After the meditation we sat and chatted. I didn't have to say anything, everyone had felt my energy. We were then asked to sit with a piece of one of the other people's jewellery in our hands and relay any messages that came to us. I had never done anything like this before but when I sat with a chain in my hand I got such an intense pain in my ear that I had to put the chain down. The pain stopped. I had no words though, but shared my experience with the chain's owner. One week later my friend told me the necklace owner's granddaughter was rushed to emergency the night of the meditation with a ruptured eardrum. Had I not mentioned the ear pain I experienced on holding her chain, she might have treated it with Nurofen when in fact it needed urgent medical attention.

For a few months previous I had visited the doctor with heart rushes. I didn't know what was happening to my body and was put on a monitor for a few days to test my heart rates. All tests came back normal and I was relieved.

I share this story because my mindset had a part to play in how much this impacted on my life. The emotion I felt while I was at the meditation was something I could not ignore. It shifted my perspective on life and in turn was instrumental in implementing change in my life.

What should I think about during meditation?

'The point of mindfulness is to learn to observe thoughts instead of getting caught up in them, so try to allow thoughts to come and go without getting lost.'
Oli Doyle

Live your dream now, not in the future

There is a golden rule when it comes to attraction. You ask for it now, you feel like you have it now and you will manifest it now in this moment, then it will create your future. The key to this is to believe it in the *now*. It is a *fake it until you make it* type of attitude. Feel it now to become it later.

One of the key elements to this being successful is to embrace the journey of manifestation. It is important not to live in the future or for the future, it is most important to live and embrace the magnificence of the now.

Feeling the essence of something while setting a clear intention is an all-powerful approach to manifesting.

I have tested this approach and it is totally achievable. One fundamental element is that you have got to make your actions align with those of your future self.

The tools you need to achieve this are:

- Confidence
- Humility
- Peripheral power switched on
- Clear intention
- Stamina
- Courage
- Belief

To create a dream life you must not only plan for your future, you must live in the present. The future is always ahead, whereas the now is where the action takes place.

It is important to have your nearest and dearest on board. If they are more of a brick wall, there are ways of overcoming that without a visit to the divorce courts. But do let them know what your intention is so they are aware of the purpose for your distraction.

In 2010 I decided to set the intention to write a book. It was the most bizarre thing for me to choose to do as I had just had my fourth child, but because I had become increasingly aware of some powerful signs that presented themselves to me at the time I kept an open mind.

I had always deep down wanted to write a book, I had even paid for a comprehensive writing course. My tutor mentioned I was a philosophical writer and the funny thing about that was that I had no clue what that meant at the time and had to Google it. I was really impressed with myself and embraced it as it was something that came naturally to me.

The first sign was that some of my blog posts had been picked up by *Universal Mind*. The producer connected with me and asked if she could publish some of my articles in her monthly magazine. Secondly, I was watching the TV program *The View* and knew I was to watch the next five minutes of the show.

There were two special guests on that day, a reality TV couple who had publicly had many miscarriages through IVF. Whoopi Goldberg stopped the show and turned to the woman saying, 'I am going to tell you what I tell all of my friends when they endure this painful loss. You endured this for a reason, you are not on the right path in life. This was a visitor coming to tell you to get on the right path and your gift will come.'

That moment was like an epiphany for me. Two and a half years earlier I had endured a double miscarriage. It was the saddest experience of my life but it did knock me back onto the right track. I felt compelled to share this realisation with others who needed to hear it. It was an all-consuming feeling. I wrote a blog about it and it was published on the website I was writing for at the time. Then something came to my attention that I couldn't get out of my mind. It was NaNoWriMo, an annual writing competition where you pledged to write 50000 words during November. Broken down this was 1667 words a day and at the end you would have a book. I was filled with the possibility that I could actually do that.

I told my hubby my intentions and I had his support so I signed up. I was two days out from beginning and hadn't got a book in my head to write about. I sat down and wrote *The Visitor* on a page and all of these ideas came flooding out. In no time at all I had twenty possible chapters, some characters, a possible plot and theme but no specific genre, simply the *Knowing* that I had to do this. So armed with the will I found a way, and thirty days later I had written 51000 words. My NaNoWriMo graph shows that every day I wrote 1667 words. I know consistency was key to me completing this dream. I had the biggest sense of achievement. I had taken action and worked hard to achieve my dream.

I had worked the Law of Attraction and didn't even know it!

What I had also realised was that I did it with loving intention. My heart was one hundred percent open and it was a very heart-centred project. When I used the Law of Attraction and my loving intention, magic happened. This has come to be the essence of how I have made so much magic happen in my life. I focus on what is amazing and within my control and I embrace it with all of my heart.

Living in the now and making the most of every mindful moment guarantees we will have many more magic moments in the future. Believe me I have tested it so many times! I don't want to wait until the future to be happy, I want to be happy now so I make sure I express gratitude for everything I have, because I am truly grateful for all of my blessings. I one hundred percent believe that when we embrace the magic in our now, we will have more magic than we know what to do with in our future.

Mighty Mindset

There are so many elements that come together to create your mindset. All so complex, no two minds are the same. As with a snowflake there is an elusiveness of similarity.

There are many different types of mindset. I would like to focus on three that are applicable for attracting a dream life. *Growth Mindset,* an *Open Mindset* and one that I have created myself, a *Magic Mindset.* These are the mindset traits of winners who will do what it takes to achieve their goals.

Growth mindset allows people to thrive during some of the most challenging times in their lives.

Imagine for a moment meeting a challenge and seeing it not as a challenge but as an opportunity to learn something new, as something to conquer! This mindset is one of an entrepreneur, space traveler, gold medal athlete, explorer and instigator of change. Quite often challenges set us back but with a growth mindset the challenge to be surpassed allows for limits to be exceeded and new ground to be discovered. It takes courage and a deep connection to purpose to make this happen. Quite often a heart-centred passion is close to the core of the intention. Again, I suggest that loving intention is the most powerful of all intentions.

This mindset perspective is often considered reckless because there is no clearly defined plan for how the task will be executed. Trusting that all will be revealed along the way takes courage and a deep sense of *Knowing*. This is the Law of Attraction facilitated at its best. Set the intention and allow the path to be determined by what opportunities present themselves on the journey.

Do people with this mindset believe anyone can be anything, that anyone with proper motivation or education can become Beethoven or Einstein? No, but they believe a person's true potential is unknown, even unknowable. That in fact it is impossible to foresee what can be accomplished with years of passion, toil and training.

Why do so many people choose to play it safe? Why are there not more people brave enough to embrace the unknown magic mindset? Do people not believe?

In researching this book I came across a principle called *The Two Per Cent Mindset*. This mindset is where I believe some Magic resides. It saddened me to think that only two per cent of the population embraces it. In this mindset is freedom, the opportunity to feel alive every day and discover your dreams.

The Two Percent Mindset is being perceived as a revolution by some. So what is it?

Individuals who take a chance, seek risks, say yes to new opportunities, and because of this mindset, they succeed!

- This small percentage of people have the following traits:
- They go for their dreams
- They embrace the unknown
- They get excited
- They like change
- They live without limits
- They believe in unlimited abundance
- They take action in spite of fear
- They get the most out of life
- They feel fulfilled
- They choose happiness
- They explore new things
- They are confident
- They will plant many seeds, nurturing those that take root.

In comparison the traits of the other ninety-eight per cent can fall into any of the following:

- Aspire to be like everyone else
- Try to fit in
- Crave stability
- Aim to survive, not to live
- Focus is on getting by
- Play it safe
- Often have regrets
- Will settle for less
- Often procrastinate

I totally tick all of the boxes in the two per cent mindset. I am delighted to reside there and even though it can be tiring I wouldn't change it for the world.

However, there is a new type of leadership taking place. It excites me to share that there is a shift and we are transitioning from a Transactional Leadership module to Transformational Leadership.

In Joshua Millar's article *Goodbye Transactional Leader. Hello Transformational,* he discusses the transition of mindset within the big corporations where leaders are changing from a 'do what I say' type of leadership to a 'do what I do' type of leadership because the old fixed mindset is hindering progression and innovation. This requires a total mindset shift from the majority of the organisation but it seems to be happening that people are more comfortable following someone who leads the way through their actions rather than their thoughts. Text book leadership is fine because knowledge is key, but couple that with a courageous leader who goes in pursuit of what they believe in and to me there is no comparison.

So faced with the choice of living a dream or being safe, know that it isn't so scary in the two per cent but it is okay to choose the stability of the ninety-eight per cent for you and your family. Yet it doesn't have to be so black and white, you can create a grey area just for you.

Exercise

What's your magic?

Prioritise what it is you want in an ideal self-focused world. In this exercise you have permission to be free from all commitments. You do not have any other priorities other than yourself.

I am a decisive person. I follow through and support myself with love.

Notes

Everyone can benefit from being mindful of their rigid thought patterns; an open mind gifts freedom.

KAREN MCDERMOTT

SECTION 2:
PERSPECTIVE POWER

Success is:

_____

Your life experience can be influenced by one simple mindset adjustment. Your definition of success can have a direct impact on who you aspire to be.

I will share with you my personal definition of success at the end of the chapter but I would like you to write down, right now what you define success to be for you!

Our perceptions of success are influenced by childhood

beliefs, the school we attended, social circles or the emphasis we have on financial wealth. These are all learned beliefs and can be altered with some challenging thoughts.

Have you ever met people and just not 'got' them, or wanted to think the same way they did but it was not something that came naturally to you? Know that it is possible, you can train your brain to think differently, but initially it will take effort before the more free-flowing subconscious way of doing things takes over.

The key to this is to become mindful, not to over think, and to act upon your intention to achieve the change you desire.

Peripheral perspective

When you hear this saying, what comes to mind?

Peripheral power is the ability to see the wider picture, to embrace opportunities as they come from unexpected sources.

I have discovered that quite often we set an intention and then have a rigid plan in place of how the intention will come to fruition. I have news for you. That is not how the Law of Attraction works.

It is your job to set an intention and then act upon the opportunities that come.

I would not have built Serenity Press up to what it is today without having my peripheral power switched on. I set the intention to publish books and trusted I would be guided through each step and I was. I could never in a million years have predicted the journey Serenity Press has taken. Every incremental step was taken out of a *Knowing* and a desire to let it grow organically. Every time I needed to upskill I faced a challenge and set out to learn what I needed to so that I could reach the next step. It takes money to grow a publishing company and I am delighted I have taken the approach of offering services to raise the funds needed to grow my business. This takes courage, determination and trust to achieve.

Just before an interview about the Serenity Press new release *Writing the Dream*, Cheryl Akle from *Better Reading* magazine asked me a question that made me realise why the business has made it.

'Karen,' she said as we sat chatting on the rooftop of her hotel in Perth, with its wonderful perspective on the city, 'it takes money to run a traditional publishing press. How do you do it?'

No one had ever asked me that before, but I knew Cheryl had an insight into the publishing industry and I had better have a good answer. So my on the spot response was to tell the truth. 'Yes it does, Cheryl and the fascinating thing is that every time I needed to raise cash flow for the business an opportunity would occur and the cash I needed would be raised. Where there is a will, there is always a way.'

At the time I answered this question we were waiting for our shipment of *Writing the Dream* to arrive from Shanghai and it was late. We were not going to meet our deadline but somehow I knew it would be okay, and it was.

Peripheral power is another super power that some people may take for granted and others may not know how to use. By seeing the wider picture you will not miss opportunities for advancement.

Anything is possible

'If you want to achieve you have got to believe.'
Karen Weaver, Job Buddies

This quote is taken from a children's book I wrote called *Alphabet Job Buddies*. It was the first thing I ever wrote for my children and it has been on a journey. It has a jingle that goes like this:

You can be whatever you want to be, if you try very hard then you will see that you can be so happy and your heart can be filled with glee.

My children still sing this jingle even though years have passed since I first introduced them to it. It gives them a warm feeling and they know I wrote it for them.

Believing in yourself is something we gift to others, especially our children, but do we do the same for ourselves? Do you expect belief to come from an outside source? When you shift your mindset slightly to realise that the belief first needs to come from within, it is then that you will start the ball rolling towards success.

You have the power, don't give it to someone else.

Anything is possible!

The only limitations are those we impose on ourselves. I have tested the Law of Attraction many times safely within my personal limitations. I am an adventurous person at heart and as my motto is, *Where there is a will there is always a way,* I am open to many possibilities.

In 2015 I realised I had been so busy having babies and building a publishing press that I hadn't been back to Ireland to see my family since my move to Australia in 2008. I set the intention to get home but did not know how this would materialise. Knowing how the Law of Attraction works I didn't stress about that, I set the strongest loving intention that I could and nurtured that seed. I identified what my biggest block was and I set out to unblock it, in a loving way of course. I always find that when you choose to unblock in a loving way there is the possibility of damage limitation.

My mum hadn't come to visit when I had my sixth child for a few reasons, one being that she was still regaining her strength from having half of her lung removed (she is the strongest woman I know!). I simply had to see her but the reality was that I had five children under ten and my husband was busy working away. I wasn't prepared to wait another few years so when I saw there was a Qantas sale I did what I could to secure flight tickets in my price range to get us to Ireland and back and it happened. I set the intention and followed it through and it was happening. I actually turned it into a business trip as time and circumstance aligned to allow magic to happen.

During this trip I met with the newly appointed Earl of Crom Castle to chat about a potential writers' retreat. Within the next year I was back in Ireland hosting the retreat at the castle. It was the most amazing experience and a really good example of how you can make the Law of Attraction work for you if you set the intention and act on the opportunities that present themselves.

Key to a magic mindset

What is magic for you? Is it beyond your wildest dreams or is it something you can reach? These are two totally different mindsets. Magic resides in the mindset with hope, the one that sees possibility not distance.

- Not being too hard on yourself when setting an intention that doesn't come to fruition straight away.
- Being aware that when you do set a big dream-focused intention, things around you need to shift so you will need to be willing to allow that to happen.
- Keep your energy high.

When I set the intention of writing a book there are things I need to sacrifice and make the important things work in a different way. I re-prioritise my life for the duration of writing my book to allow the space in my busy life to let in the magic of time. This also relaxes my mindset, allowing creativity to flow. The biggest thing I compromise on is a tidy house. When I am writing a book my house is a mess, as you can imagine with five children from two to twelve running around with Mummy distracted. I eat a lot when I am writing so they don't suffer food-wise but they do have lots of outside play in the garden, beach walks and movie times as I often write books when they are on school holidays. That may seem totally irrational but it works for me as I don't schedule in work on school holidays. I am home-based so anything I do need to do I can do from home. It is during these times that my heart sings.

It is however not a great time for cash flow but that's okay because I am confident that one day I will hit the mark and write a million dollar book or create a million dollar business. In the meantime I will make it work and enjoy the process and in doing so my children are learning the dedication it takes to write a book. I hope they will also learn how to tidy the house properly some day and I won't have to stress when someone knocks at my door in the school holidays.

I am sharing this insight because it is how I have shifted my mindset to work around my circumstances and that has allowed me to achieve so much. When we become more adaptable we won't feel like we are sacrificing too much on our quest.

I have lost count of the times people have said, 'I don't know how you do it.' The only reason I achieve what I do is because I set my intention and follow it though. When things begin to shift around me I do my best to make sure my priorities are not compromised and I have to trust that the rest will be fine. I also pursue a lot of things with loving intention, therefore minimising any external negative impact. They also happen faster. It is a fact that when you pursue something with loving intention it comes to you faster. The heart channel has the quickest magnetic force because when we open our hearts to receiving, it radiates from every aspect. Everything I pursue, I do so with loving intention.

Exercise

Name one life goal you have always wanted to achieve. Is it still on your bucket list?

Honour that dream by filling out the Dream Table on the next page.

Now may be the time to take action and plant a seed of possibility that you will achieve this in your life.

I suggest you sit with your dream for a moment and be honest. Don't push to fill in the lines, write what comes to your mind first.

Dream:

_____

Can	Can't
_____	_____
_____	_____
_____	_____
_____	_____
_____	_____
_____	_____
_____	_____
_____	_____
_____	_____
_____	_____

Now feel love for all the things you can do. Read each one you have listed and be grateful that you can see them as potential catalysts to achieving your dream.

Know in your heart that you deserve to make your dream a reality. You are the only one who can nurture this seed. You are the chief gardener in your destiny garden. Are you up for the job?

Now it is time to turn all your *can'ts* into *cans*.

You can take as much time as you like with this exercise but I do suggest you make the time right now or very soon to see the possibility before you; to safely think outside the box and take each one of these blocks and transform them into a positive. This exercise is life changing.

*I practise Mindfulness
in every moment.*

Notes

Mindfulness is being constantly aware of our thoughts, our surroundings, our bodies, our feelings, other people — everything in that moment only!

AMANDA GORE.

SECTION 3: KINDNESS KICK

Part A. Kind energy

Kindness doesn't cost anything but it can be the best investment you will ever make.

I cannot even begin to share the number of times kindness has paid off for me. It is a mindset choice that is truly magical. The energy created through being kind is gentle and so inviting for others. It is detected from a distance and appreciated on so many levels by others.

For the giver, happiness is never far away from kindness.

> 'Happiness is not something readymade.
> It comes from your own actions.'
> *Dalai Lama.*

Kindness may not be the sexiest of all actions but don't underestimate its potential to have a profound impact on your life.

I really enjoy being kind. I like to be a ray of kindness into someone's day. It helps people reconnect with others instead of withdrawing. Kindness is what communities are built upon. *Be kind to thy neighbour.*

I grew up in a close-knit community until I was nine. Neighbours would watch out for each other's children and there was a sense of compassion and unity within that community. It's an amazing feeling to gift someone because it is not something that is expected, it is something that is gifted.

The sense of community is not as freely given now. I believe that stems from fear and not taking the time to get to know who your neighbor is anymore. I am blessed that I live on a street in Western Australia where my neighbor hangs bags of vegetables over the fence for my family. He gives without expectation of return but I know that someday I will repay him tenfold for the random acts of kindness he gifts our family. When he does it, it makes my day and I am so grateful. And as gratitude is one of the best ways to navigate onto the flow of abundance it is more than vegetables that he is sharing with my family.

I am a great believer that world peace can be achieved through kindness. Love is stronger than hate but quieter. When random acts of kindness make the news a wave of kindness ripples through society and yet news channels often choose to share news that is negatively focused, news that spreads fear and sadness. I find it sad that good news is not as commercial.

If we focus on what we can do ourselves, no matter how small, it will have a ripple effect that will soon become a tsunami of kindness that has the potential to instigate positive action in our world.

If everyone adopted a mindset that love, compassion and kindness were superpowers and set about using them daily, imagine how different the world would be. It's a nice prospect.

Part B. If like attracts like, kind attracts kind.

> 'The game of life is a game of boomerangs. Our thoughts, deeds and words return to us sooner or later with astounding accuracy.'
> *Florence Scovel Shinn*

Even though we cannot control what comes into our life we can choose what we act upon. When we react to something an energy is created from that action. When we purposely choose to set our mindset to respond in a kind and loving way it is amazing to watch the response of others.

This mindful approach works really well with children, they are very receptive to it and flourish because of that.

Some adults are less open to the concept, quite often due to their life experiences. When you are approached with negativity and respond with kindness, quite often the response to that will be criticism but know that you will have left a lasting impact, something for the person to think about. It may even be a catalyst for them to look at their behaviour. It is a human instinct to defend against threats so responding with kindness and compassion often has to be consciously learned but it is really worth it to watch it in action.

> 'Kindness is always an option. Choose it.'
> *Dalai Lama*

The Dalai Lama lives and breathes kindness and compassion. The energy created from that has an immediate impact that makes the haters be still. He often speaks of the importance of discipline to live a peaceful life.

'A disciplined mind leads to happiness,
and an undisciplined mind leads to suffering.'
Dalai Lama.

A lot of what he shares is filled with divine wisdom and comes from a source of kindness. It is worth exploring the Dalai Lama's quotes if you wish to embrace kindness.

Remember, what you give out is often what you get back. Would you choose kindness if it was an option?

Part C. Why kindness will get you far.

It is your responsibility to share with others that which you have learnt in this lifetime. You never know whose life you could change just by being you.

I have been involved in the business community for years now and one thing I have come to recognise is the sense of unity in the women's business sector. Women tend to support and uplift each other. I have watched women in a position of influence recommend another woman's product, creating a demand and making a positive impact on that person's business.

I love watching random acts of kindness like this and have often wondered why this is more evident among women. I have come to recognise that women don't fear being vulnerable. They are prepared to embrace the journey with their intention set, and trust in their knowing that they are on the right path.

When I joined the Ausmumpreneur network I was astounded by the support and encouragement I received from people I had not even met. Yet we connected on a deep level that has ignited deep friendships. In 2015 when I attended my first conference, that was made possible through the kindness of a gift of a conference scholarship, otherwise I would have chosen not to attend. It was the best thing that happened for my business and because of that I give so much back to the Ausmumpreneur community as I have a strong heartfelt connection to it.

These ladies are kind in the way they approach others and it has assisted them to create an amazing tribe of like-minded women who raise each other up.

I thrive on being kind to others. It makes me feel so good to have made someone else feel good. Not everyone feels the same way but that's okay as I know that by giving in this way, I will inspire someone else to give in another way. I love inspiring others and having a positive impact on someone's life. I am not afraid to reach out when I feel someone needs a helping hand or a hug. Rejection comes with the territory but more often than not my kindness is embraced with a refreshing sigh and a grateful heart. It all stems from loving intention.

> 'Be kind whenever possible. It is always possible.'
> *Dalai Lama.*

When I give kindness I do it without expectation and yet it often comes back to me tenfold. I know my success stems from the kindness I have put out into the world and how that is embraced by so many people. My intention shines bright and my fearlessness in pursuing my dream is also embraced. Being kind is at the essence of who I am and I know it has brought me this far.

Be mindful that if you are scared about something good it is quite often an indicator that it matters. No one has ever achieved greatness by waiting on the sidelines.

> 'Take into account that great love and great achievements involve great risk.'
> *Dalai Lama.*

Exercise

Dedicate one day to random acts of kindness. Send a kind note, smile at a stranger, offer some help or do anything you feel is kind.

Journal your day below.

Thinking before I speak is Mindful magic.

Notes

The world is full of magic, waiting for us to learn how to use it.

W.B YEATS

SECTION 4:
LIVE LOVE

Part A: Law of love

'The truth that for our life one law is valid — the law of love, which brings the highest happiness to every individual as well as to all mankind.'
Thierry Dufay

The Law of Love is the greatest power of all. When I first began researching the Law of Attraction I came across studies stating that it was firstly known as the Law of Love. When you open your heart centre, the potential to receive is increased tenfold.

I have been reading *The Law of Love & its Fabulous Frequency of Freedom* by Jasmuheen and the following passage connected with me:

When the human heart is filled with love from self, for others and for our planet, this heart focus automatically puts them into the stream of the Law of Love and allows more grace to flow into their lives, it also allows for an easier activation of their original freedom codes which are held in their light body matrix.

These words hold so much knowledge on the way that love projects out and magnifies back to us something magical. Is there any more important reason to be mindful, to be more loving?

I have chatted about the time in my life when I was numb to feeling. Hand on my heart I can tell you that I attracted nothing good into my life during this time, but when I woke up and became a loving person again my life turned around. I know it was a love of life, my family and myself that made amazing opportunities flow my way again. I realised that if the door is firmly closed, how can the magic of life get in?

I now choose to live in love and it serves me very well. If you choose to trust in the power of love then you will see the fruits of life grow too. Every single thing you pursue with loving intention will flourish because love makes things grow beautifully. It is not for the faint hearted; living a passionate life comes with its own challenges. It can be confronting for some but those who support your passion will be gifted with a heart-centred connection.

Living a life filled with love is a choice, it can come from the most basic of upbringings. Love is something that is in a heart and it doesn't cost a thing.

One vision that comes to me is how happy some of the poorest of cultures are. Are they are happier because they have fewer choices? Is it because they have lower expectations and therefore are grateful for everything they receive? Is it because they have more time to let magic into their lives?

Whatever it is, they have what most people aspire to achieve and that is happiness.

'When one door of happiness closes, another opens; but often we look so long at the closed door that we do not see the one which has been opened for us.'

Helen Keller

Part B: Love, the healer

Love is the most powerful healer of all.

The one thing I keep coming back to for this is Louise Hay's *Heal Your Life*. This book is life changing.

It is written through the channel of loving intention and at the back there is a reference section that details the spiritual reasoning for physical ailments. I was shocked when I discovered the reasoning for lower back pain is financial worry. Funnily enough my husband suffers from severe back pain at times and he has become accustomed to now asking, 'What have you been spending?' I did set on a quest to get him to say the affirmations that would ultimately eliminate the negative thought pattern at the source of the problem but found that you can lead a horse to water...

Another explanation that intrigued me was that cancer is caused by holding on to resentment as it eats away at the spirit just as it eats away at the body. Dr Siegal who wrote *Love, medicine and miracles* suggests that traumatic events are precursors for cancer and he asks, 'What happened in your life in the two years before diagnosis?'

Louise Hay has had first-hand experience in curing her cancer by putting her philosophies to the test. She developed an intensive program of affirmations, visualisations, nutritional cleansing and psychotherapy to cure herself and in 1984 she released *You can Heal your Life*. I am a great believer in the power of the mind to heal. I also believe in the loving intention the medical profession has put into creating cures and performing surgeries, and that combined with the power of positive thoughts, healing will be at an accelerated rate. We are not all Louise Hays with such self control and natural knowledge so it is best to take advantage of maximum healing options.

My father suffered two strokes one year apart shortly after I moved to Australia. I had just had a baby and moved to a new country and felt the distance intensely at the time. My father has always been a very strong man and to think of him weakened crippled my heart. I have always been very close to him also, which intensified it even more. But amazingly, one year later he hopped on a plane and came to visit us. This was the best thing ever! To see how much he had healed was amazing. My dad has always been a person who 'gets on with it' and who has a bubbly character. He rarely got sick and when he did he would quietly heal and move on. Another year later and he had a consultation and MRI that astounded the doctors. His brain had fully healed, there was no sign of any scarring. Now my grandfather had early strokes and he sat by a fire all day and the strokes became something that defined him, but my dad wasn't prepared to do that. He wanted to drive again, he wanted to heal so much so he focused all of his energy on it and he did. He didn't do it alone, he had our whole family sending love and helping out as much as we could.

Love is an amazing healer. The energy created from the loving vibration emitted is all powerful. Look at a mother's love, it has the biggest healing potential of all. If my kids graze a knee or are really ill with a temp, it is my healing hugs that make them feel better, accelerating the healing process.

So the next time you are unwell and head off to the doctor or the chemist, consider also exploring the emotional trigger that caused the health problem and look at resolving the root of it so it doesn't present itself again.

Good health is my divine right. I am open and receptive to all the healing energies in the universe. I know that every cell in my body is intelligent and knows how to heal itself. My body is always working toward perfect health. I now release any and all impediments to my perfect healing.
Louise Hay affirmation

Part C: Let all that you do be done in love

It's written in the Bible, so why do we not instantly do it? I expect it is because we are human and our minds are so complex. We like to over complicate things for ourselves and that's fine, but imagine a life where there was more space and things were simpler and much brighter. That is a life led through the heart.

You know those people who wear their hearts on their sleeves? I am one of those people but I have learned how to instantly shield myself from negativity. You know that Wonder Woman shield, ready for battle at any moment? It helps you when facing fearful situations because you will have confidence in the *knowing* that your heart is safe.

There is no pain as intense as a broken heart.

I know this first hand but I refuse to live a life fearful of experiencing this pain again. Instead I chose to be brave and put loving energy out into the world, fearless of the consequences. Love is confronting for some people but with those who embrace it, I have deep lasting connections.

The key to this is intention. I am passionate about the intention of people I meet. I often find myself silently questioning their intention for pursuing or saying things. I do have empathy for people who have been through a lot and who have underlying issues that lead to choosing negativity, but it comes back to the matter of choice. We can choose what we let define our lives, we can choose love, we can choose happiness or we can choose the opposite. It is all a matter of choice. I went through a rough time in my life and I became an introvert for a while, it was my choice and something I needed to do at the time. It was a dull place for me and I never felt at home there but I did emerge from it and chose to live a love-filled life that serves me so well. I could have chosen a very different path and I am so glad I chose love.

The easiest way to begin, if you haven't already, is to become more mindful of your intentions and in turn your actions. The act of giving is something special indeed and when executed without expectation it releases the disappointment that may follow, while also enhancing the experience of heartfelt gratitude when it comes.

It makes so much sense to pursue everything with loving intention. The results will be more than you could ever imagine and will come to you so much faster. Love is my go-to intention and so it comes very naturally to me. It can be the same for you with a little mindful focus.

I suggest you start small with things that are familiar and safe and then begin to find the courage to push the boundaries safely out of your comfort zone. You can even experiment and have fun with it all. I did. It makes it all so different when you do it with the *Knowing* that you are safely surrounded by love.

Exercise

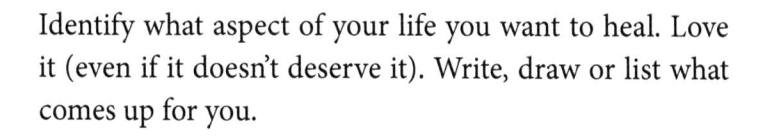

Identify what aspect of your life you want to heal. Love it (even if it doesn't deserve it). Write, draw or list what comes up for you.

Mindful creativity is the key to blessings and miracles.

Notes

*Where there is a will,
there is always a way.*

KAREN MCDERMOTT

SECTION 5: CONFIDENT CASH

Part A: Absolute abundance

'Money makes the world go around.' Well no, it doesn't, love does, but if you love money then you will have plenty of it.

You see, what you love most is what you will receive most of. If you are like me, money will not be the top of your list of priorities when in fact it should be, because with money I can make magic happen in my life, the life of my family and the lives of others.

We all deserve to experience financial abundance in our lives and we all can, but most of us don't want to sacrifice what we have in abundance (family love, lifestyle etc) to get it. However you don't have to. If you shift your mindset to becoming more open to receiving in a softer way, you can make a difference and not feel like you are compromising your life but enhancing it in a positive way.

This can be done through affirmations that will gently assist you in creating financial energy that will open up the channels of receiving money.

I have recently tested this and it worked. Being in the publishing world, projects need financing. I am usually good at moving forward and have a positive outlook on cash flow and building a business, but at this point I felt stuck and the cash had stopped flowing, which can be really tough for a business needing to do big things. I was also busy and doing lots, so my focus was scattered. I decided to take a day off and refocus my energy on creating wealth for my business. I sat with the loving intention of growing and I read the following affirmations from *The Secret* wealth app:

I am happy to give because my abundance is limitless.

I attract all that I need to bring forth my success.

I am a wealth creator.

I am using money to bless my life and other people's lives.

Every day in every way my wealth is increasing.

I am excited by other people receiving money.

The Universe conspires to give me everything I need.

I thank the Universe for all the prosperity that is mine today.

I am financially thriving.

There is an abundance of money and it's on its way to me.

I am receiving more money today.

I always have more money coming in than going out.

I love money and money loves me.

I am generous with money.

I am excited to see where more money is going to come from next.

The key to having more money is to feel like you have more money right now, in this very moment. This can be really tough if you are in debt or money is limited, but I can promise you that if you commit to being mindful about the money energy you are sending out into the Universe, your money story will change.

After one day of doing this I was receiving enquiries for new projects, had new ideas coming to me to act upon and even money that was outstanding found its way to the business.

This is relevant for business and home life. I suggest you put energy into making debt not feel like debt. The debt trap will only be a trap if you allow it to be.

Be grateful every day for everything you have. No matter how small it is, feel gratitude for it. Gratitude has instant access to the flow of abundance.

When you want to accumulate wealth, fill your mind with wealthy thoughts, feel wealthy when you think about money. Trick your mind into feeling wealthy and wealth will follow. The Law of Attraction works by giving you what you think about most, so it is important that when you think about money you are emitting a positive abundant energy to allow it to flow freely to you.

Part B: Money Mindset

An abundant mindset that is mindful of the Law of Attraction is when someone consistently thinks prosperous thoughts irrespective of their actual situation and in turn manifests prosperity in the future because 'like attracts like'. Conversely, if a person consistently thinks they are poor then that will be their future experience.

One example comes from my LinkedIn friend Lisa Nichols, who is part of the film *The Secret*. She shares that *'Every time you look inside your mail expecting to see a bill, guess what? It'll be there. Each day you go out dreading the bill, you're never expecting anything great, you're thinking about debt, you're expecting debt. So debt must show up...it showed up, because the Law of Attraction is always being obedient to your thoughts.'*

Feeling happy and grateful for the money you already have is the fastest way to bring more money into your life.

It is a total shift in perspective about money and is well worth the effort, not only to increase financial wellbeing but to enhance emotional and health wellbeing. It is a win/win scenario and that is why New Age thoughts have been embraced wholeheartedly.

It can be quite tricky to manage if you are not a full believer. But when you entrust some of your energy towards it and begin to see results, it makes it easier to realise it is not a coincidence that you are actually using the power of your mindset to create money magic in your life. When opportunities you would never have considered start coming your way, it is then that you will truly begin to trust that there is a powerful connection to the energy flow of abundance. You can even play around with it and have a little fun. The key is to gain confidence and watch as it happens. But always remember it is your job to set the intention of wanting more money in your life. It is your job to feel wealthier, allowing it to flow to you, but it is not your job to know how it will present itself to you. So be open to opportunities and if they feel right for you, then go for it.

'People who have drawn wealth into their lives used The Secret, whether consciously or unconsciously. They think thoughts of abundance and wealth, and they do not allow any contradictory thoughts to take root in their minds.'
Rhonda Byrne.

Part C: Money is on its way

When I was doing my Advanced Law of Attraction training, one of the modules introduced us to a formula for True Abundance and I would like to share it with you here.

It states that on the whole being rich or being poor is not the answer. The ultimate goal should be: *To become abundant, mentally, spiritually and financially.* Goals should include the whole picture, not just the financial, otherwise you will run the risk of not knowing what it truly means to become abundantly fulfilled.

You may have blocks when it comes to attracting money, but you can change how you think about it and consider that true abundance is really about positive growth and giving back to ensure the cycle of abundance continues. You will be attracting money to make your dreams and maybe even the dreams of others come true. The formula is, when you think about abundance, think of every aspect of your life, not just the financial, and each will complement and support the other.

To align yourself with abundance you must first become mindful that whether you like it or not, you are the conscious creator through the action of the Law of Attraction and your physical reality is determined by the contents of your heart and mind. Your emotions will create the feeling that will attract the abundance for you, so every feeling you have, you need it to be reaching its fullest potential.

And remember that your dreams and aspirations should genuinely matter to you, not to others. Because true abundance will only be achieved if it is you that truly becomes happy with the desires and outcomes you have set for yourself. That does not mean that if you and someone else have the same desire, you both can't manifest it successfully together. It means that it is important to not only do it for them but also for yourself. Your greater good will be grateful that you did.

Here are five tips from the advanced Law of Attraction course by Joe Vitale and Steve G Jones.

1. You have to allow money to flow into your life one hundred percent.
2. You must not doubt your ability to manifest any amount of money at any point in your life.
3. You must believe that there is nothing wrong with having material wealth.
4. You must desire material wealth but you must not be resentful of those who have already manifested their financial abundance.
5. Deep down, you must truly believe that you are completely adequate and that you deserve all the wealth that you want in this world.

Exercise

Create your own vision board. This can be done with pictures, words, on a computer or on a physical board. Feel what it is like to have each item you add. Every time you look at it, feel good about having it.

Breathing in and breathing out helps me to rebalance.

Notes

I practise mindfulness every day.

The entire universe is a great theatre of mirrors.

ALICE BAILEY

SECTION 6:
INTUITIVE INTENTION

Part A: Power of intention

Setting an intention is like pressing a green button on a goal and giving yourself permission to go for it! It is often beneficial to let loved ones in on the deal, along with those in your social media circles, as your peripheral power will be switched on to pick up on opportunities that will assist you to achieve.

I watch others setting focused intention all of the time and they succeed against all odds. It is second nature to me. I will give something my all if my heart is in it. If I have no interest, then it is hard for me to engage. You will get the best results channeling through loving intention. If you don't do it automatically, you will be glad to know that it is something you can access mindfully. If you put the effort into it a few times, it will feel more natural.

I continuously set intentions and move towards achieving them, even sharing the intentions in my circles so that those around me understand where my focus will be for the foreseeable future. Setting intentions is how I got to where I am today. Each week in the Ausmumpreneur group the beautiful Peace Mitchell asks, 'What are your intentions for this week?' The question itself is an instigator to focus on three main things that week. These three things are often part of the bigger focus but each step in itself is important. This is always a powerful way of letting those around you know where you are at.

Writing this book takes focus and although my world is not falling down around me I have had to consciously make room and focus on writing it. My way of focusing is writing each morning. During the day if I get the chance is a bonus but often I use that time for research.

Setting the intention is taking the first big step on the road to achieving your goal. Be inspired, take action and get ready to love the journey to receiving.

'Whatever you can do, or dream you can do, begin it. Boldness has genius, power and magic about it. Begin it now.'
Johann Wolfgang Von Goethe

Part B: Fabulous focus

The Power of Focus and the Law of Attraction cannot be separated. Whatever you are focusing on, you will eventually attract into your life.

Focus is the key to success. Embarking on the quest of penning this book has taken a lot of focus for me. I set the launch date quite some time ago and although I was committed to writing this book straight away, life and work priorities had to come first. My days became so busy that my treasured writing time at night and in the morning was overshadowed by the must dos. Don't get me wrong, I love what I do. Publishing books is my passion and I love building my publishing company into the magical business it is. My problem is that I prioritise other things over my own needs, but I did it, I made the conscious decision that everything else would have to wait until I got this book to print because it was important.

Do you see what I did there? I set the clear intention!

This is a valuable mindset trick. Clear space, give yourself permission to let the magic of inspiration in and take action.

Writing this book is one of my personal goals for this year and I don't have to jeopardise it. I tend to work best at the last minute because I am totally focused on the goal of completion but to be honest I am not totally sure how it will turn out. I will do my best, and as one of my mottos in life is *'Where there is a will there is always a way'* and I have the will, so I will find the perfect way for me. All of my knowledge tends to come to the forefront of my mind when I work this way. When I was studying Humanities with the University of Ulster I always completed my assignments the night before they were due to be handed in.

I know a lot of people couldn't work like that, but that's how I worked and it helped me pass. I was able to fully focus on the task, I had all of the information and the desire to complete it was way more than the desire to sleep and so with my magical combination I pulled it out of the bag. It is not for everyone but it worked for me and failing was not an option.

'Successful people maintain a positive focus in life no matter what is going on around them. They stay focused on their past successes rather than their past failures, and on the next action steps they need to get them closer to the fulfilment of their goals rather than all of the distractions that life presents to them.'
Jack Canfield

Part C: Journal progress

Journaling is very powerful when you are evolving, not only for looking back to see how much you have progressed or to identify patterns. It can used as a vehicle for deepening mindfulness as it helps to clarify and refine thoughts and emotions and will bring you more into a present mindset. Very much like meditation, journal writing helps to clear the mind by releasing emotional clutter onto a page. You will become a witness to your past behaviors, which will then pave a way forward with clarity.

Your journal is a great companion wherever you go. It can be used as a resource for observing shifts in your inner world and outer behaviour. When we journal, it gifts us the opportunity to reflect on past events and see how far we have evolved in our story. Journaling is also a powerful tool for releasing emotion. When we allow our words to flow freely we get them out of our head and onto paper, which often gifts clarity to situations that may have been causing distress. It makes a situation more tangible than something our mind has stored.

>'If you are clear about your goals and take several steps in the right direction every day, eventually you will succeed. So decide what it is you want, write it down, review it constantly, and each day do something that moves you toward those goals.'
>Jack Canfield

Recently I found a journal I wrote in throughout 2009. It was amazing to see how far I have come but also nice to see where I was at in life. It's funny as my memories did not reflect what was written in the book and it helped me see that year in a more positive, transformational light.

I created five journals with quotes for each week that are based on a fifty-two week structure. I love using them for gratitude, attracting new things, writing down things I am inspired about, positive things that happen in my life and setting intentions.

Exercise

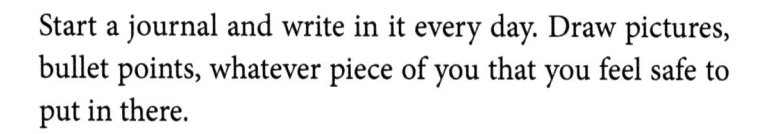

Start a journal and write in it every day. Draw pictures, bullet points, whatever piece of you that you feel safe to put in there.

I create firm foundations for myself and for my life. I choose my beliefs to support me joyously.

Notes

*A Knowing is a feeling thing,
not a thinking thing.*

KAREN MCDERMOTT

FINAL: GREAT THINKERS

There are many great thinkers in this world of ours. Here are a few who have touched my life and how.

Rhonda Byrne: Her book *The Secret* was the book that opened my eyes to the power of our thoughts and energy. Her story from a very low point in her life to her realisation is very powerful. If you haven't checked out her books or video I suggest that you do.

Louise Hay: This woman created an empire around her and her book *Heal Your Life* was a pleasure to include in my life. My first book *The Visitor* was published through Balboa Press. Although it wasn't the greatest experience, I turned it into a positive and founded my own publishing press through the knowledge I accumulated. Time and circumstance aligned with me on this one. Check out Louise Hay's work and prepare to feel loved and inspired.

Amanda Gore: This beautiful ray of sun shone into my life in a happiness bubble shortly after I had founded my publishing press. Of course I really wanted her to write for me but she was so busy at the time. I have recently reconnected and was delighted to discover that she is still shining her rays of joy on others. I know we will connect at a speaking event someday, maybe even share a stage. I would love you to check out this amazing lady if you don't already know her.

Elizabeth Gilbert: I have chatted about how I connected with Elizabeth Gilbert when she came to Perth International Arts Festival. Her energy is relaxed and yet electric. I love that she pursues her own journey and is filled with wisdom. If you don't already know her I suggest you check her out.

Oprah: I crossed paths with Oprah in a roundabout way. I heard she was coming to Perth in December 2015 and kicked into an instant mission to get a gift basket of books to her and I did. I went to watch her at Perth arena that night and although she didn't give the callout my heart hoped for, I received so much from being in her energy. Oprah is amazing. She is a prime example of what it is to be born into something and then choose that there is something more for you out there, and once you embrace the magnificence of the journey, anything is possible. If you don't know Oprah you may be hiding in a cave somewhere so go check her out straight away.

*I am mindful of my breath
in each moment.*

If you can dream it, you can do it.

WALT DISNEY

QUOTES TO LIVE BY

- From every negative situation there is the potential for a positive outcome.
- Where there is a will there is always a way.
- Everyone has a story to share.
- When time and circumstance align, magic happens.

Each one of these quotes has been significant in my life and the path I have chosen to walk. They were signs that I became aware of that held the answers I required at that time in my life.

Have you got quotes that have been relevant in your life? Write them below.

_____

_____

_____

Don't worry about being original, be authentic.

ELIZABETH GILBERT.

SUMMARY

Your mind is the most powerful asset you have, it creates the story of your life. We all have one life and one story to tell. What do you choose for your story? After working through this book would you still answer these questions the same way?

What is mindfulness?

_____

_____

What is magic?

_____

_____

Notes:

I would love for you to visit my Facebook page and share your answers in the pinned post where I will choose a winner every month for one year after the launch of this book.

I have profound inner strength and serenity.

Whether you think you can or think you can't, either way you are right.

HENRY FORD

COLLECTION OF ARTICLES

Our Universal Minds

It has become more widely recognised that our thoughts create things. Those of us who open ourselves up to the possibility of being more than just one physical being in one lifetime are becoming more of a universal thinker. It may seem out of this world initially but when you open yourself to the possibilities you will soon discover that it is easier than you first perceived. In fact, it soon will become second nature.

Energy

Everything in the world is energy because we all derive from atoms which are ENERGY! At the beginning of the evolution of everything that exists you can be sure it began as an atom. As humans we are affected by the energies that surround us. The energies we release can be picked up on, especially the frequency of others if they are tuned into us through emotional connection.

A few days ago I had a very unsettling feeling and couldn't shift it no matter how hard I tried. My kids picked up on it and they were more cranky than usual and anything I did just didn't work, my computer wouldn't even switch on. I went to work that evening and I could feel myself pulsating like a beacon. I ensured that my external demeanor did not portray my inner feelings yet still my friend came to me and asked if I was okay as she felt very uneasy for me. When I got home and checked my messages, I had messages from close friends and relatives near and far asking if I was okay. They had all tapped into and picked up on my energy like energy hackers. This is just one little tiny example of the greatness that is the universal communication network, no wires required.

Understanding

It can be quite an overwhelming thing to realise that through our thoughts and feelings we create our own future through the Law of Attraction. We don't need to feel like that, we just need to understand it for the simplicity that it is. As I understand it, the more things I do to make me happy, the more things come my way to make me happy. I remember once doing a personal development activity in which I had to write down twenty sentences beginning with 'I WANT'. Then one by one I had to delete them from that list until I only had one left. I found it hard to pick between the last two as one was about the happiness of my son and the other, which I did pick, stated:

'I want to always be happy, because when I am happy those who love me are happy too.'

The lady who facilitated the group was overwhelmed when she read it.

So many of us seek externally for happiness. Many people search in this way for a lifetime but it is those of us who realise that true happiness comes from connecting within who live a fulfilled life. All of the answers we need to guide us through our life reside within. When we listen to our inner spirit guide we cannot fail because it is then wisdom finds us; wisdom that we never knew we had begins to shine through.

Universal Gifts

We are all sent messages from the Universe that we can pick up when we open our internal receptors. We put out our requests for what we want our life experience to be and the Genie of the Universe will show us the way to achieve our heart's desires. All we have to do is be aware of the signs. These messages may come through conversations with others, a serendipitous encounter or you may simply be drawn towards something that will lead you to your goal or you may have a moment of inspiration. Whatever way you are guided, it all starts with you being aware of the signs the Universe sends your way.

We will however receive these messages clearer and stronger when we stand still; this may be through meditating, resting or praying, whichever way works for us at the time.

Avoiding unfortunate events

Since becoming more aware I know that I have avoided many unfortunate occurrences. The only way I can describe this is that a signal will be sent to me in the form of a warning. For example, if I am rushing about and everything seems to be going against me, it is for a reason. I no longer stress about it because it is happening for a reason. Maybe that red traffic light is preventing me from having an accident or maybe by the kids not wanting to go somewhere it is stopping me from having an unwanted encounter. All I know is that since I have begun reacting to the universal signs that guide me I have had a less stressful journey through life.

When you are going against that grain and travelling down the wrong path in life, the Universe will let you know. When everything is going against us it is worthwhile reflecting on past events. Should we keep pushing forward because anything worth having is hard fought? For me, I would take on board lessons learned and wait for the way to be revealed. Life is the adventure that we want it to be and the Universe will help us live it the way we want to should we so choose.

Opening ourselves to receiving.

There are so many people who are not open to receiving. They give so much but don't feel worthy enough to receive the gifts they so rightly deserve. We first have to want something in order for it to manifest into reality. It is not for us to determine HOW we will reach our destination - that is the domain of the universe; it is however, our duty to clearly request what we want to experience in life. When we have done this then it is up to us to open ourselves to receiving and act on the signs sent to us. A simple process that can often be mistaken for something far more complicated.

Challenge this today.

Clearly request something you want. Shout it out loud, write it down or tell someone else. Then feel what it is like to have it, close your eyes and believe that you have it. Keep the faith that the Universe will deliver by express courier exactly what you want, it IS on its way. Act on opportunity when it comes to you. At least once a day take a moment to feel what it is like to have it, get excited, smile from ear to ear, and jump up and down. Why? Well because by feeling it, it will bring it to you quicker.

My life is filled with endless magical moments.

The Spiritual Law of Attraction

Over the past few years I have become increasingly fascinated with the whole concept of metaphysics or *The Universal Law of Attraction,* which is the term most of us are more familiar with. I began to explore and embrace affirmations, especially those of Louise Hay, who has guided many people gently through the process of transforming their thoughts to assist in bettering their lives and healing themselves physically and emotionally.

Then there is the phenomenon of *The Secret* by Rhonda Byrne. This book and movie really connected with me. It is more of a factual guidance that reveals something fascinating and intriguing. The power of our thought and the history behind the power of this knowledge really sparked something inside me and I started to implement conscious thought processes in my life to test if it worked.

As I am a spiritual person and have made a transformation within that has connected deeply with my inner spirit, I knew any conscious alterations in my thought process would also have to complement the peace and fulfilment I have achieved through my inner connection.

I started off small. If my day was not flowing well, I would stop for a short time and readjust my thoughts to a more positive mindset. Every time I did this my day would change towards being a more positive and enjoyable experience. The energy I was putting out there was the energy I was receiving.

I also used the same principle with my children. When they were going crazy and getting on my nerves I would readjust my thoughts and remind myself they are just children who need loving guidance. By playing up and messing about they were just being healthy kids and testing their boundaries. If I responded in a furious over-reactive way, then I was affirming to them that their behaviour was acceptable as I was responding in the same way and they would then continue on their rampage. When I took a few moments to adjust my thoughts and feelings and consciously send love to them, I found that almost immediately they changed their behaviour. The same principles applied when my husband was having an off day.

The point I am making is that immediately in that one moment I was able to apply simple changes that made a positive difference in MY life.

I put together a vision board and events began presenting themselves to me that led me towards achieving my dreams. I discovered that part of the process of receiving everything we want from life is to be open and aware of the opportunities that come our way after we request something, while also using our heart and being guided by our inner spirit as to whether the choices we are making are right for us.

Spirituality

If we ask for something and things shift to enable us to receive it and our heart is affirming that it is right for us, then don't deprive yourself. It is right for you! Our inner spirit is our guide and it will not allow us to drift too far off our path without letting us know.

When we as individuals connect with our inner spirit we activate our strongest intention. When we connect this intention with our desire for something to manifest, whether it be emotional, spiritual, material or any other medium, we activate our strongest power.

Passion

When we approach things with a true glowing passion we will receive far more quickly. A lot of things I do, I do with passion and a whole-hearted true intention. Things happen for me very quickly. I discovered I was passionate about becoming a writer. In two and a half years I wrote two novels, more than sixty articles and set up a rapidly growing publishing business - and all of this while being a mum to four. Every single step of this process I was guided towards what I needed to do in each moment. I am now finishing my third novel and my heart is singing.

Negative influences

I have come to realise, through my own experiences and other interactions I have witnessed, that the people we connect with regularly can have a huge impact on our mood and therefore influence our thoughts and life outcomes. Do you put up with a negative influence in your life because the person is a family member or you work closely with them or for some other reason? If you do I strongly advise that you try your best to limit as much as possible any interactions with them. If this seems impossible then try your best to make any interactions with that person more positive.

You can also consciously create an energy shield around yourself to block out the toxic energies this person projects by taking a moment to centre yourself within. Doing this will create a stronger centre of balance for you. Follow that by imagining you have a protective shield around your whole body and nothing this person says or does will alter the way you are feeling right now. Keep yourself conscious that you are not going to let your feelings be altered by the negative influences the other person expresses.

Religion and attraction

Many people access their ability to attract things through their religious practice. Prayer is very powerful as often it is not only one person but many people all focusing on the one outcome for themselves or another. There are many different religions, all of which can influence the power of thought through their practice.

By watching the movie *The Secret* I realised the power of combined, focused thought is covenanted as it has the potential to alter the pattern of life for us all, it is that strong.

When large groups of people get together with the same passion and intention the energy emitted is on a transforming level and the Universe must do its job in responding. This is not only the case in religion but also for worldwide campaigns, rallies where a lot of people gather together for the same cause. The internet can reach so many and the energy combined from all over the globe at a specific time has monumental potential to shift energy frequencies.

Loving Law of Attraction: The Mirror Effect

Stop for one moment! Think about what you are doing. What type of energy are you projecting? What do others see and experience from you? The only way to know this is to look in the mirror. This simple act will allow you to experience the outer you that others experience all the time.

You will be fascinated to know that looking at yourself in the mirror is one of the hardest things for a lot of people.

Love Yourself... Do you love yourself? If you don't truly love yourself (warts and all), then how can you expect someone else to love you? Can you honestly look in a mirror and say to yourself 'I love you!' with all of your heart? This simple act can turn out to be one of the most liberating things you will ever do in your lifetime.

Louise Hay affirms that this is one of the most wonderful things you can do for your self-love. Jack Canfield, author of the *Chicken Soup for the Soul* series, often talks about 'The Mirror Exercise'. It is a self-love exercise that is designed to be completed every night.

Give it a go...

Get ready for bed.
Stand quiet and alone for a few minutes.
Find a mirror and stand in front of it.
Really look at yourself, deep into your eyes. It may feel awkward at first but try to stick with it, it will get easier the more you do it.

Examine yourself closely. Your eyes, your skin, your

forehead, your nose, your mouth, your body (if the mirror is big enough); examine everything and try to only think positive thoughts about yourself. (If you are brave enough to try it naked, go for it! If not then don't pressure yourself because you can still get powerful results).

When you are ready, look lovingly into your eyes and tell yourself 'I love you' and add your name. This may make you feel uncomfortable at first and don't be hard on yourself if it does. Honour your emotions by letting them be and when you are ready, later on you can reflect on them and release them. It is important to do this because every time you do, you heal an old wound.

Reflect on your day and think of at least five things that you appreciate yourself for and say them out loud to yourself. They can be as small or big as you like but they must be positive.

Connect to your loving core and flow love and compassion towards yourself the best that you can. When you truly open your heart you will feel this physically like a ripple or rush in your heart.

Focus on the things you love about yourself and tell yourself about them. Think of your reflection as your best friend who needs to hear some positives right now. We are all our own best friends and when we take time out to realise that, magic can happen.

To finish, look deeply into your eyes (the gateway to your core) and say 'I love you' and mean it with all of your heart. Again, embrace the feelings this brings to the surface and see this process as a strength.

When you love yourself for who you are – not wanting to be someone else, just doing all that you can to be your 'best self' – you will make mountains move in your life!

This reminds me of when I was training to be a community drama tutor. At one of the workshops, we all walked around a room and when the facilitator said stop, we had to stop and stare into the eyes of the person closest to us. I could not believe my reaction, and neither could the other participants. I had come to know everyone really well over the duration of the course. We had been going away to different locations all over Ireland and Northern Ireland for almost a year together, we were cast together in plays and were working very closely. I was one of the super confident ones. I would be the one having the fun and leading a lot of the groups.

This workshop was the biggest challenge for me. I found myself closing my eyes, blinking or giggling and looking away – anything to hide my utter discomfort with the activity. I couldn't do it. I couldn't let anyone look deep. I think I could more easily have run around the room naked! Why?

Of course, looking back now I know all of the answers but at the time, I didn't. I may have always been the popular one and the joker but that was all a charade for what was going on inside, and that was a lot at this time. I didn't loathe myself but I certainly didn't love myself the way I should and I didn't want anyone to see the true me by looking so deep. It felt as though I was being invaded, it was really uncomfortable. I learned a lot about myself through this exercise. Would you have been able to let someone look into your eyes? Could you look deeply into someone else's?

Just like the mirror, what you give out is what you will receive in return! It is the Law of Attraction and when you execute it with all of the love in your open heart, this is when you will experience the all-powerful Spiritual Law of Attraction. It makes you shine your divine light out into the world so that you will attract divine magnificence into your life.

Loving Law of Attraction: A tortoise or a hare?

We have all heard the story about the hare and the tortoise. The hare brazenly boasts that there is no way in the world a tortoise could beat him in a race. This is to his own peril as his cockiness was soon proved to be his downfall. Of course the moral of this story is that being steadily consistent until the end will overcome the fast show-off hands down. We have all heard it. 'Slow and steady wins the race.'

The hare got brazen and was filled with ego whereas the tortoise was humble and consistent. For me, the tortoise is way more likeable than the hare. Who do you choose? Neither of them considered at any point that they would not reach the finish line, but the hare expected to come first. The tortoise didn't, he didn't mind the prospect of not winning but was happy when he did.

Which do you think would win a marathon? Endurance or speed? A car wastes more petrol when it speeds around, stopping suddenly and speeding off again at traffic lights and roadblocks. It may even lose control if the driver is not paying enough attention on the road ahead and the situation. Think about it; this process can also be applied to how we approach life, love, relationships, jobs, challenges...

'Going slow may not be as exhilarating a ride but it will always get you to the finish line.'

When I sat down to write my first novel, if I had started with the intention of blasting out as many words as I could, I would have run out of steam. Instead I made it to the daily recommended word count and each day I still had inspiration to keep going until I made it over the line thirty days later. Applying this to other aspects of my life, I know that when I blast into something, I quite often hit a brick wall. When I embark on the task with a realistic goal in mind, I take each step knowing I am one step closer and wiser.

Maybe the pace of the tortoise doesn't work for everyone, I certainly can't ever imagine the hare going at the same pace as the tortoise, it would not be in its nature; but in life we can train ourselves to slow down.

Pros and cons of being a tortoise: At the tortoise's speed the exhilaration of the race is not at the same level as the hare's but the tortoise has the opportunity to enjoy the journey, not just the finish line. The tortoise gets it all...he gets to bring his home with him and yet still take part in the race.

Pros and cons of being a hare: Fulfilment can be harder to achieve and the next race is never far away. Always after the goal, never enjoying the journey.

I used to live my life at the hare's speed; I was always exhilarated but never fulfilled! Life decided to give me a jolt that made me live one day at a time and since then I have lived at the pace of a tortoise. I now have time to look around me and embrace life as I still pursue a finishing line; it is so much more fulfilling. I have, on occasion, noticed the hare try to sneak back in, trying to coax me to run again, and sometimes I do for a while but nothing beats the tortoise's pace for me!

There are jobs that require fast thinking and action and that is fine once balance is found in other areas. Life goes fast for many of us. Sometimes if we don't keep up we may feel like we will be left behind but I can assure you that if you keep making progress towards your goal, no matter the pace, you will catch up with the hares at some point because they will have to stop to rest.

In relevance to the Law of Attraction, if you live the fast-paced life all of the side effects that come with that will come at a fast pace too and your body may begin to suffer as a result (something worth considering).

Are you a tortoise or a hare? What would you prefer to be?

Loving Law of Attraction: Ask – Believe – Receive

You can be whatever you want to be.

Life is not so much about finding yourself as it is about creating you.

Why is it that as children we are encouraged by our parents, storytellers and society to dream and believe that anything is possible, only to be drawn away from this momentum as we move into adulthood? Why is it, as adults, many of us turn our back on the magic of life to embrace a more socially acceptable, duller reality as we advance through the years? Is it all a process? There are those who are lucky enough to reconnect with their inner child at some point during their journey, and this more carefree, fun approach to life can bring about a more enjoyable experience of existence during this lifetime. I am not saying we should all start acting like children, but we can learn a lot from connecting on a more consistent basis with the magical dreamy believer – our inner child.

Take a step back!

Take a step back for a moment to look at what you have become in the now and momentarily ask yourself, 'Are you happy with who you are?' Does your heart sing from time to time, reminding you that your body, mind and spirit are aligned? Do you feel fulfilled? If the answer is no to any of these questions, then what have you got to lose if you consider opening yourself to alternative possibilities? This does not have to be a dramatic life-changing event. It may simply be doing something that you hadn't considered before and discovering you actually like it; or promising yourself to save some special time just for you at the end of every day; or even beginning to take steps towards fulfilling a personal goal. Each little positive step can soon become a momentous positive journey.

Get rid of that mental block!

Think about something you would really like to have in your life, something that will enhance your experience of life but won't jeopardise anything precious that you already have. Believe it is possible for you to fulfil the dream of receiving whatever it is. Think about it often; make yourself feel like you already have it. Think of it as mentally preparing yourself for receiving. Make it real in your mind and feel it wholeheartedly and you will make it real in your reality. Do not let doubt create a blockage in your mind; have a clear vision and let the light shine on it.

Anything is possible, you just have to believe.

Attraction

By truly believing, you will attract opportunities that will help you create your best future. It is important to become more aware of signs and when opportunity comes knocking, answer the door! Be mentally prepared to be brave and take the plunge towards your heart's desire. People around you will start to believe in your dream when they begin to witness what you are attracting your way. You need to believe in order to attract, that is your job in the process. All you have to do is be aware and don't turn your back on the opportunities that will help you make your desire a reality. If you turn your back on these opportunities then how are you supposed to take the next step along the journey of receiving? It is a process and we all have some work to do to achieve. If we choose not to then we don't want it enough or it is not right for us. Regret is not an option. If it is meant to be, the opportunity will find its way to us again.

Do your best with what you have now and it will attract more to you in the future.

My attraction

I live the perfect life for me. I know the Law of Attraction is hard at work for me every single day. I know that I have attracted to me everything good, and even some of the not so good. I love that I have the power to influence my own life in the way I choose. My life may not be what someone else would choose for themselves, nor might it have turned out exactly as I thought it would, but because I have always remained open and followed what I felt was right for me it has paid off and I am living my dream. I would always advise anyone to stay true to themselves when they are feeling confused about what road to take. Connect with your intuition, it will guide you! And when you know what it is that you want, then put it out there and act on every opportunity that you possibly can that will bring that desire one step closer to reality. I am very grateful for everything I have been blessed with, I treasure it wholeheartedly!

Become your own Master

It is good to remember that we are the masters of our own life. It is a life we have been gifted with by a higher source, a source that will bring to us our mind's requests. When our requests come from a positive loving place, what we receive will also be positive and loving and vice versa.

The Law of Attraction, when consciously connected to our inner spirit, can be a strong generous amalgamation of power that can work to meet our highest potential. When we allow our heart to sing and have faith, that is when our heart's desires will be delivered. Anything is possible!

We cannot control everything that occurs in our lives but we can control how we choose to react to it. Try to remain conscious in every moment and to pause before a reaction, because nothing is so urgent that it need not take a moment to address. The moment to address action can be used to instigate a response through a loving heart, and with the truest of intention only the purest outcome will ensue, if that is how we choose to live our life.

'When we live our life through love we are choosing to live our best possible life.'

By living a life of passion we attract those desires to us at a faster pace because when we live with passion, we feel with passion and the Universe provides us with what we are most passionate about.

It is a must to focus our passionate energy on what it is we want to manifest the most.

Think it, feel it and believe it!

Loving Law of Attraction: A negative path

It is important to understand that just as you can attract many positive things into your life, you can attract negative things too. This can be an overwhelming responsibility of thought for many of us, but it is a fact. The way we can help control it is through our feelings. A chain of events that happened to me instigated this thought process.

I began to feel an energy shift and instead of dealing with it as I usually would, by doing something nice for me that makes me feel good such as writing, spending some time with friends or going for a walk, I found myself being consumed by a strong unsettling feeling. This unsettling feeling was picked up on by my very in-tune friends at Soul Sistas Healing as cards began jumping out at them with messages for me. I then requested a reading that stated someone would slyly betray my trust.

Of course my mind went into overdrive. Before I knew it I had conjured up all sorts of scenarios in my over-active imagination (attracting allsorts to me), but the main thing was that a gloomy shadow of negative feelings engulfed me and it would not shift. I just didn't have the strength to shift it – I was tired and doing a lot. So I chose not to react, I chose to let it pass over. Whatever it was going to be, I was going to have to deal with it, I had reached a level of acceptance. Once it didn't physically affect any of my family I didn't mind, I could deal with it. I began to simplify things around me for the short term.

The next day my husband phoned to tell me he had had an accident on the freeway but no one was hurt. I was so relieved.

The negative sensation was still there, yet dimmer than before. A few days later my negative emotion and the negative journey of another crossed paths. My Cash Card was stolen and the person went on a shopping spree. I don't usually have cash in my account like that but circumstances following the incident a few days earlier had led to there being money in my account and that person was guided to it. Also the shops he visited facilitated his deception by not being suspicious, but then again, this is the Universe providing the desires of the other person.

You see, the Universe had aligned all of these things to make this happen not just for me but for the opportunist that was focused on achieving their goal – with passion.

The key to conquering the situation before it accelerates to the outcome is not to over think, it is to make yourself 'over feel'! Over-feel **good feelings**. When we feel with passion we are manifesting things at a faster pace. We have the ability to realign! This is a power we are all born with. I know now that I should have realigned when I got the warning signals. If I had listened and acted in a positive way, all could have been avoided. I may have done one small thing that would have changed the course of this happening.

Acceptance

Everything happens for a reason. Sometimes we can explain why…sometimes we can't. Sometimes we need to take action… sometimes we don't. All I can recommend is that you listen to your intuition. Be aware of how you are feeling. If you are feeling unsettled then do one small thing that will accommodate a realignment and then FEEL GOOD ABOUT IT!

The Law of Attraction is all about learning. You may navigate onto a negative path, either your own or stumble onto someone else's. Either way it is worth remembering that YOU have the power to move forward at whatever pace you decide to. You have the power to choose how you deal with each scenario. You choose whether to allow someone else to dictate how you should deal with something, or you listen to your intuition and move forward more equipped with knowledge and experience to perhaps prevent similar happenings in future. Wise words state that 'prevention is better than cure' and the best way of doing this is by listening to our intuition. It is our spirit guide and it will let us know if something is wrong. It will niggle us until we listen and act. It has our best interests at its core, it works for our greater good!

Try your best to find a positive in every negative situation – there is always one if you take the time to look.

> 'From all negative situations is the potential for
> a positive outcome.'
> Karen Mc Dermott, *The Visitor*

Loving Law of Attraction: To catch a fish!

No matter what you pursue in your life you will be best rewarded if you are patient. Think of the fisherman. If he wants to catch a big juicy fish he will first find out where the specific fish is positioned and then he will prepare himself for the long haul.

Picture it now…he makes sure he has the best bait to attract the fish to his line, and then HE WAITS! You will never see a fisherman hop into the water and make a fish bite his line. It doesn't work like that. The fisherman has in his mindset that he may have to wait all day to make the catch of the day or it may happen on the first bite. He may have to weather all sorts of storms but the one thing that never changes is his faith and belief in the possibility of the outcome. While he is waiting he may imagine what it would be like to finally catch the perfect fish. Little does he know that by imagining he is manifesting.

When that bite comes, that's when all the hard work starts. Then he has to reel in his fish successfully. There may be a tango of differences during the process but when that fish is caught in the net, the exhilarating feeling that ensues is worth it. That fish is a deserved reward for the fisherman.

Yes, if you want to be a fisherman you have to focus, be patient, believe it's possible and work hard. The same rule applies for everything worth having in life.

Many times I have achieved the big catch by using this principle. When I chose to move to Australia from Ireland, I focused on the goal. I was patient during the process (which took two years), believed with all of my heart that it could happen and that it was right for me, and then I worked really hard placing myself in the position to receive my dream (preparing, setting up and settling in). By the time I had received it, it was already a reality for me!

Now, and in my future, I continue to apply this principle to different aspects of my life because I experience the benefits it has. I love to write and I have published some of my work. The more I cast my line in the right places the more chance I have of achieving my big catch. Now that, for me, would be exhilarating.

Don't underestimate the process of WAITING.

We have to wait for things for a reason. Our mindset needs to adjust from dream state to reality based during the waiting period. If we received something the moment we imagined it, it would be mind-blowing! It is the time we have to believe that it is possible and the time to consider if the outcome is right for us. Are you sacrificing too much to receive? Is there room for something new to enter your life? This is the time set aside to consider all of these things; before you receive you may need to spring clean your life to make room for it. The fisherman is sacrificing time and energy for the momentary exhilaration of the catch. He had to make room for that time but what is he missing out on? Was it worth it?

This process of attraction can also work for negative thoughts too. If you focus your energy on something that you don't want to attract and you believe that it is possible, you are indeed working against your greater good. Always try your best to focus on a positive outcome!

Finally...DONT GIVE UP! When you 'put it out there' be open to every possibility of it coming to you. Just like the fisherman catching his big catch, he cannot control when that is going to happen. He can put himself in the best position, be prepared for any scenario and be willing to wait it out!

'Good things come to those who wait...and believe...and think positive...and are prepared to work hard.'

Are you reaching your true potential?

Mindfulness is all about having your peripheral vision switched on to allow the magic in and keep the crap out.

The time is now to change your mindset, change your life.

Focusing in the present gifts me an abundance of mental clarity.

Go within or go without

One of the best things I have ever done in life is to go within. Since doing this a whole new treasure trove of wisdom and fulfilment has found me. Don't get me wrong, I still encounter life's challenges from time to time, but they now don't seem as challenging because I am in the knowing that no matter what happens, it is more than likely happening for a greater good in the long run.

I know for a fact that when I am on a frequency of happiness and contentment, more happiness and contentment comes my way. Every now and again I may put a request out there for something I desire and then I do nothing other than act on the opportunities that present themselves to me. The universe is in motion, bringing to me whatever it is that I have requested. This is not always a good thing because if I truly feel and believe that something not so good is going to happen, then that will find me also. Also it is worth bearing in mind that we must be careful what we wish for as the sacrifices we may have to make to make way for the delivery of the desire may not be worth it in the end.

However sometimes negatives happen to make way for more positives. Or maybe sometimes we are being tested by a messenger to receive a gift bigger and better than your everyday requests.

Going within does not necessarily have anything to do with religion, although many people use religion as a vehicle to guide them through the tough times and to send off more frequencies of happiness, thus attracting more joyous moments. It is logical when you think about it. Also, positive energies combined are very powerful. For the greater good of humanity, if more and more groups come together with the aspiration of positivity, then positive things will happen.

Others may access meditation for a more connected, intense experience. Stillness and an empty mind help cleanse the soul and get rid of the entire toxic gunk that has accumulated there over time. A poem by Jodi Davis sums it up in a few short but inspiring words.

Go within or go without
by Jodi Davis

Life is a school with one lesson to learn
a major in Love is what I'm talking about.
You won't find it out there in the desert
You must go within or go without.
We spend years crawling in dry sands
scorched by the desert's burning heat.
Until we look inside our hearts
we're left yearning for something we can't see.
Fed by an ego afraid of being forgotten
it whispers that it knows the way
When you turn from the voice of ego
Love reminds you, you're already safe.
You can only discover the sweet embrace of Love
through learning to love your Self.
Then you will find it easy to begin
now you are free to love everybody else.
We are all 'one' in reality
when you find pure Love you'll have No Doubt.
Yet you can make this discovery only one way
you must go within or go without.

Another thing that I discovered when I went within was forgiveness. This I discovered and embraced as it is truly a gift to me and no one else. Through forgiveness I have opened so many doors that I had shut over the years and it gives me a glow inside when I think about it so I know that forgiveness is good for me.

The Glow

The glow is like my spiritual guide. It lets me know when I am making the right decision. It can be mistaken for excitement but when you learn to recognise the glow it will be an invaluable way of being guided by your spirit. I have realised that this is what Jesus was talking about when he referred to the Holy Spirit. As a child I used to think it was a dove with a shining light beaming behind it sort of experience, but I now know that this is an inner glow guiding us through life and must be respected and listened to if we wish to travel the right path for us in life.

Love

Love is divine, love is healing, and love is all powerful. I could go on all day about love. It frees us to connect with others. When we open our heart chakra we are inviting and sharing ourselves with others, which I believe to be the true path to fulfilment. When we feel true love for another it is healing. Have you ever thought about why a mummy kiss is all healing? I know I have, us mums pump so much love into that kiss that it actually helps our children heal. I never cease to be amazed at the power of this healing love. When we believe and the child believes that all will be well then it will, because no fear or doubt is harboured. I feel that this also applies to all aspects of healing and life in general. We all have the ability to heal and be healed through divine love and unwavering belief.

Strength

When I say strength I don't mean the physical type, I am thinking more of strength of character. Because we are human we all have strengths and weaknesses, that's what makes us interesting. Strength comes from within and helps us through tough challenges that we all face at some time or other throughout life. It is our strength that keeps us sane and keeps us filled with hope and trust that all will get easier and that life is good, even though it may not feel that way sometimes. It is our strength that helps us bounce back, maybe even wiser than before we stumbled.

Inspiration

We all have a creative side. When we don't express our creativity in the way that is unique to us all then we will find it hard to ever be fulfilled. For me creativity comes in the form of writing and drawing, I just love expressing myself this way. Other people use music, sports and other mediums as a vehicle of self expression. But all in all, it comes from the same creative source within to begin with and just a different avenue is explored to express it. The world would be a boring place if we all expressed our creativity in the same way, wouldn't it? I like to think of creative expression as the rainbow that beams right around the world sprinkling droplets of love and hope and happiness and making way for the sun to shine.

An affirmation found me when I was in the middle of writing this article and it encompasses the essence of what I feel.

"I allow myself to trust in the process of life and what I need comes to me easily and effortlessly."

My advice if you want to go within is, don't force it. It will happen naturally when you are ready. You need to slow down and listen to yourself. Don't have miraculous expectations in your mind. My experience is more of everything clicking together and a feeling of safety and awareness. So don't forget: Go within or go without.

KAREN MCDERMOTT is an award-winning entrepreneur, multi-genre author, publisher, mentor and renowned speaker. She's also an advanced Law of Attraction practitioner which means she teaches people how to attract anything they want into their lives.

Through the art of manifestation, Karen has created a highly successful publishing business, financial freedom and a life she loves - all in the space of a few short years. Karen is an expert in helping others achieve success in all areas of their life and through her mentoring and support, you can too.

Karen believes we all have the ability to attain any goal or aspiration we want. By focusing our energy on the positive aspects of our lives, instead of the negative, is when the magic happens. By following Karen's step-by-step manifestation process, you'll be able to rewire old thought patterns so you can start living your dream life.

God has shown me that it is a scientific fact that gratitude reciprocates.

MATTHEW MCCONAUGHEY

THE KNOWING

You have read many times throughout this book about what I call a *Knowing*. For many years I have spoken about the *Knowing* I have and more recently I speak about it freely in my workshops and presentations. Every single time I get the same reaction as most people in the room have an 'Aha!' moment at the same time. That's something special, right? Here's my definition of a *Knowing*:

A *Knowing* is not a thinking thing, it is a feeling thing.

When you come to realise this and its potential, you can truly connect with the essence of your life. When you have the ability to connect directly to the essence of your *Knowing* your experience of life will change instantly. You will feel more in control and if you connect this internal superpower to the brain power you also have, possibilities are endless.

It takes courage to connect with your *Knowing*. But the rewards of wisdom, guidance and a life led with purpose are bounties worth the pursuit.

Often, it is when we are at our lowest point that our *Knowing* reaches out and gives us hope. We have nothing to lose and so we entrust it in hope of salvation. It rewards us by shining a light through the darkness.

I think I have always been connected to my *Knowing*. It comes naturally to me to make confident decisions based on what I feel is right for me. They may at times seem totally irrational considering where I am at that particular moment in my life, but when I am called in a certain direction and my heart is saying 'Yes' and my head is saying 'Hold on a minute', I know I can trust my *Knowing* to guide me to make the right choice. There is an affirmation I used to say in times of doubt that would assist me to connect with my *Knowing*.

I make decisions based on principles of truth, and I rest securely in the *Knowing* that only right action is taking place in my life.

Imagine for a moment if we were taught in school how to connect with our *Knowing*. That each of us has an internal guide that works at all times for our greater good, something that works only to serve us. How wonderful would that be!

In my next book *The Knowing* I will share the stories of people who have lived through their *Knowing*. It is stories like these that reach down deep inside, connecting to your soul. These stories have the power to shift a perspective and life will not be seen the same way again. So watch out for *The Knowing*. I hope that through reading this book you are gifted with the insight required to live your life to its truest potential.

Watch out for my next book in the series
The Power of *Knowing*

A Knowing is not a thinking thing, it is a feeling thing.

THE Power OF KNOWING

K P WEAVER

Each day brings new magic.

FULL SERIES COMING SOON

THE *Alchemy* OF LIFE *Magic*
7 Master Gifts to Live Fearless and Purpose Driven
K P WEAVER

- THE *Power* OF KNOWING — K P Weaver
- THE *Miracle* OF INTENT — K P Weaver
- THE *Gift* IN GRATITUDE — K P Weaver
- THE *Law* OF LOVE — K P Weaver
- THE *Freedom* IN *Forgiveness* — K P Weaver
- THE *Beauty* IN BELIEF — K P Weaver

Lightning Source UK Ltd.
Milton Keynes UK
UKHW020837150121
377095UK00009B/200